Sandy Hinzelin

All beings are Buddhas
Treatise on Pointing Out Buddha Nature

3rd Karmapa

Sandy Hinzelin

All beings are Buddhas

Treatise on Pointing Out Buddha Nature

3rd Karmapa

Translated from the French by Astrid Montuclard

RABSEL
PUBLICATIONS

Original Title : Tout les êtres sont des Bouddhas, Éditions Sully, 2018

Rabsel Publications
16, rue de Babylone
76430 La Remuée, France
www.rabsel.com
contact@rabsel.com

ISBN 978-2-36017-047-0

Table of Contents

Acknowledgements 5
Preface 7
Introduction 9

Presentation of the 3rd Karmapa and the *Treatise on Pointing Out Buddha Nature* 11
A couple biographical elements 11
His work 13
Treatise on Pointing Out Buddha Nature 14
- Buddha nature is present in all beings 14
- Mahāmudrā and Buddha Nature 17
- Context 19

Translation of the *Treatise on Pointing Out Buddha Nature* from the 3rd Karmapa Rangjung Dorje 23

All beings are Buddhas 39
Introduction 41
Transforming Experience 43
Is ineffability an issue ? 44
Meditative Exploration 48
Which path? 50

First part: Ordinary consciousness 53
Attachment to the five aggregates... 54
Ordinary experience of "I" – the individual self 56
Ordinary experience of the world – the self of phenomena. 57
The causes of dualistic grasping 58
Conclusion 60
... is source of suffering 60
Mental formations 62
Saṃskāras and afflictions 63
Happiness according to ordinary consciousness 64
Aging, illness, and death 65
Impermanence 66
Endless quest 66
Conditioning 67
Saṃskāras, karma and phenomena 68
Saṃskāras and *karma* 68
Saṃskāras et phénomènes 69
Adoption and rejection do not lead to satisfaction 70

Second part : Awakened consciousness 72
The end of *saṃsāra* is possible 72
The three turnings 73
Mahāmudrā of sūtras 76
First turning: Realization of the emptiness of personal self – the state of *arhat* 78
Meditation technique 78
Moonbeams 78
Satipaṭṭhāna sutta 80
Cognitive transformation 82
Four objects of attention to deconstruct the individual self 82
Qualities to cultivate 84
The refrain 87
The peace of the individual emptiness 89
Action 91
Limits 93
Cognitive limits 94
Limited Peace and Action 97
Conclusion 98

Second Turning and the no-self of phenomena: intellectual understanding of emptiness 100
Different reasonings 100
Authentic imagination – a factor for awakening 102
The limits of intellectual understanding 103
Intellectual understanding and liberation 103
It is not a direct perception 104
Examples from Śāntideva and Candrakīrti 106
The realization of emptiness necessitates another form of understanding 108
Third Turning and the no-self of phenomena : Buddha state, emptiness, emptiness-luminosity 110
Meditation techniques 111
Recognizing the nature of afflictions 113
Recognizing the nature of sensorial objects 114
Arriving to the certainty that everything that arises is unborn 116
How to apply these instructions? 117
Cognitive transformation 119
Non-conceptual wisdom 120
The wisdom similar to the mirror or wisdom of suchness 124
Characteristics 124
Center of space 132
Wisdom of multiplicity 132
Wisdom of equality - one flavor only 132
Discriminating wisdom 133
All accomplishing wisdom 134
Phenomena are comparable to an illusion. 136
Conclusion 138
Two modes of knowledge 138
Knowledge of the absolute 139
Supreme Peace and Awakened Activity 142
The peace of phenomena's non-self 142
Awakened activity, the three *kāyas* 144

Why all Beings are Buddhas 147
Presence of Buddha Nature in all beings 147
Evolution of perception over the three turnings 147
The space 148

The qualities are indissociable from the nature of consciousness.... 150
The *dhātu,* creator 151
Causality of the transformation 152
How to explain the presence of these qualities ? 153
"We are not certain" 154
Buddha Nature and Mahāmudrā 155
Mahāmudrā's essence 156
Gradual Way 158
Deepening of experience 158
Deactivating the process of grasping 159
Conclusion 160
The coemergence 162
Emptiness and Buddha Nature 165
Conclusion 166

Translation of titles in sanscrit and abbreviations 169
Bibliography 171

Acknowledgements

My deepest appreciation goes first to my two Phd supervisors, Emmanuel Cattin (Université Paris Sorbonne) and Matthew Kapstein (EPHE), who gave me their trust and accompanied me throughout this work.

Many thanks also to K.D. Mathes (University of Vienna) for his numerous remarks and the preface of this book.

My appreciation also goes to François Chenêt (Université Paris Sorbonne) and Isabelle Ratié (Université Sorbonne Nouvelle, Paris 3) for their judicious comments.

I also thank the PHIER and the PhD School of the Université Blaise-Pascal in Clermont-Ferrand for their warm welcome and their various events aiming to promote the research of young researchers.

This work has additionally been possible thanks to help of Buddhist centers in connection with the Karma Kagyü lineage, where I have been able to meet lineage masters, khenpos, and practitioners. A big thank-you to each of them.

Finally, I thank all of those who have helped and supported me. I particularly want to express my sincere gratitude to my parents and my family.

Preface

In his *Treatise on pointing out Buddha Nature the* 3e Karmapa Rangjung Dorje (1284-1339) not only summarizes the key concepts of the standard Indian treatise on Buddha Nature, the *Ratnagotra-vibhāga* (tib. *Rgyud bla ma*), but also presents them in line with his tantric interpretation of Buddha Nature, namely that all ultimate buddha-qualities have ever been complete within one's *vajra* body. In a way typical of his Kagyü tradition, he avoids a too eternalist position by excluding that buddha qualities have no causes at all, as they naturally evolve in an everlasting momentary contiuum. Moreover, Rangjung Dorje is famous for having linked Buddha Nature with the *mahāmudrā* concept of natural, or uncontrived mind (*tha mal gyi shes pa*). This work, together with Jamgön Kongtrül Lodrö Tayé's (1813-1899) lucid commentary on it, has become one of the most studied texts within the Karma Kagyü school.

Sandy Hinzelin's French translation of this material thus is a most welcome contribution, all the more, as Kongtrül's commentary has not only been accurately translated directly from the Tibetan[1], but it is also profits from Sandy Hinzelin's careful PhD study of its historic-philosophical context. The present book will be a starting point of, and a major source textbook for, the study of Buddha Nature and Kagyü *mahāmudrā* in the francophone world.

Prof. Dr. Klaus-Dieter Mathes
University of Vienna

1 The commentary of Jamgön Kongtrül Lodrö Thayé has been translated into french. It is available in english in Brunnhölzl Karl, *Luminous Heart: The Third Karmapa on Consciousness, Wisdom and Buddha Nature*, Nithartha Institute Series, Snow Lion, 2009.

Introduction

« All beings are Buddhas ».

Each of us has therefore the possibility to become awakened, to perceive reality as it is, and to liberate ourselves from what enchains us and leads us to dissatisfaction. No one is excluded, the only condition is to remove the different veils that cover what is already there.

This situation can be compared to a person sitting on a treasure, except that the latter is buried underground. It is only by digging that we will take advantage of it, any search at the surface of the ground will not lead anywhere. Consciousness is also a treasure, but it remains inaccessible as long as perception lacks depth.

Which path is to be walked to see what we truly are? How is awakened consciousness, Buddhahood, characterized?

In the *Treatise on Pointing Out Buddha Nature,* the 3rd Karmapa Rangjung Dorje[2] (1284-1339), Tibetan master from the Kagyü lineage concisely presents Buddha nature,[3] and he gives some elements to *see* it directly. Based on this treatise and a commentary from Jamgön Kongtrul Lodrö Thayé[4] (1813–1899)[5], a phenomenological approach is offered to touch on these questions.

---

2 Karma pa rang 'byung rdo rje.

3 Sct. *Tathāgatagarbha*, tib. *de bzhin gshegs pa'i snying po*. Litterally "seed" or "heart" of a *tathāgata*, but commonly called Buddha nature. See the explanation of this term in the commentary from Jamgön Kongtrül Lodrö Thayé during the presentation of the title. On the notion of the "heart," see Schaeffer 1995, p.4-5.

4 'jam mgon kong sprul blo gros mtha' yas.

5 This commentary has also been translated in English (Brunnhölzl 2009). Even if the thought of Jamgön Kongtrul Lodrö Thayé is sometimes divergent from the one of the 3rd Karmapa, his commentary overall seems to restitute the meaning of the treatise. For an inventory of the different commentaries of the 3e Karmapa's work and the *Treatise on Pointing Out Buddha Nature* in particular, see Schaeffer 1995, p.18-21. K. Schaeffer has also translated the commentary of the 5th Shamarpa.

Presentation of the 3rd Karmapa and the *Treatise on Pointing Out Buddha Nature*

A couple biographical elements[6]

Rangjung Dorje was born in January 1284. He is also called the 3rd Karmapa, “The one who accomplishes Awakened activity,” a title meaning that he is the third hierarchical one of the Kagyü[7] lineage. Orgyenpa[8] (1230-1309) would have given him the name of Rangjung Dorje because it was the secret name of his previous incarnation – the 2nd Karmapa Karma Pakshi[9] (1206-1283). Even if he is one of the important representants of the Kagyü lineage, the 3rd Karmapa has also a strong link with the Nyingma[10] lineage and the thought of Dzogchen[11]. His father, known under the name of

6 The different existing biographies are presented in Schaeffer 1995, p.6-7.

7 bka' brgyud. M. Kapstein presents the main lineages of Tibetan Buddhism in Chapter 7 of The Tibetans (Kapstein, 2006 p. 260-266).

8 O rgyan pa rin chen dpal.

9 Karma pak shi. It is with the Karmapas that the Tibetan institute of reincarnations of great masters (tib. sprul sku – “Tulku”) was established. Kapstein 2000, p.99.

10 rNying ma.

11 rdzogs pa chen po.

Chöpel[12], was a nyingmapa practitioner. Rangjung Dorje received teachings from Kumarādza (1266–1343), Dzogchen master of the *bi ma snying thig*[13] lineage, and the influence of the Dzogchen is visible in the work of the 3e Karmapa, for example in stanza 14 of the Treatise on Pointing Out Buddha Nature. Besides, his predecessor insisted on the fact that the unique difference between Mahāmudrā and Dzogchen was their name[14].

The 3rd Karmapa studied various subjects such as epistemology[15], the Prajñāpāramitā, the Madhyamaka, the Abhidharmakośa, the Vinaya, the Bi ma snying thig, the Mahāmudrā and even the ancient and modern tantras. His biographies indicate that he also met great masters of the Buddhist tradition throughout his life in pure visions and dreams. He also made several trips to Tibet, and he went to China twice, which contributed to a greater influence from the Karma Kagyü on the relationship between Tibet, China, and Mongolia[16]. Several times, it is indicated that he chose his destinations depending on signs that he encountered. His activity extended in several fields in order to work for the benefit of others. He firstly taught a lot and did several retreats. Among his important disciples, there was the 1st Shamarpa Drakpa Sengge[17] (1283-1349) and Longchenpa[18]. Additionally, he is said to have accomplished miracles such as stopping a great forest fire in Tibet and also saving people from an earthquake in mainland China. Rangjung Dorje also contributed to the construction of several buildings – restauration of temples, construction of a bridge and hermitages, paintings in the palace of the Yuan court representing the Kagyüpa masters, and he was engaged in "mediations" in order to solve different conflicts.

In 1338, in front of an assembly of officials representing Mongolia, Rangjung Dorje declared: "Me, a yogi, I am comparable to the clouds. May all whom wish it grasp as quickly as possible the meaning of my teachings." He died in Beijing in 1339, aged 55.

12 Chos dpal.

13 Like Longchenpa (Klong chen rab 'byams, 1308–1364).

14 Kapstein 2000, p.105.

15 Sct. pramāṇa, tib. tshad ma.

16 On the links between Tibetan Buddhism and Mongolia, see Kapstein 2006, p.123-131 (ch.4).

17 Grags pa seng ge.

18 Arguillère 2007, p.49 and following.

His work

The 3rd Karmapa wrote several books in different styles and on different topics, such as the Mahāmudrā, Buddha nature, the works of Asaṅga and Maitreya[19], astrology[20], the practice of Chöd[21], the counts of Jātaka[22], songs of realization ... It is especially the texts that express his philosophical view that will be of interest to us here. Six of them are considered as important:

(1) *Profound Inner Reality*[23] (1322): this text is primarily based on the *Niruttarayogatantra*[24].

(2) The commentary of *Profound Inner Reality* (1325).

(3) The *Treatise on Pointing Out Buddha Nature (date of composition unknown*[25]) : this is essentially a summary of the *Supreme Continuum*[26].

(4) The *Treatise on the Distinction between Consciousness and Wisdom*[27] (1323[28]): he primarily relies on *The Ornament of the Mahāyāna Sūtras*[29], *Mahāyāna Summary*[30] and the *Supreme Continuum.* He presents a summarized version of the Yogācāra presentation of the eight consciousnesses and four wisdoms.

---

19 Brunnhölzl 2009, p.86. On the transmission of these texts of India in Tibet, Brunnhölzl 2014, p.81-91.

20 See Schuh 1973, pp. 34-36 (Dieter Schuh, Untersuchungen zur Geschichte der Tibetischer Kalenderrechnung, Verzeichnis der Orientalischen Handschriften in Deutschland, Supplementband 16. Wiesbaden: Franz Steiner Verlag, 1973).

21 *Gcod.* Schaeffer 1995, p.15.

22 Schaeffer 1995, p.15.

23 Tib. *Zab mo nang gi don.*

24 Nevertheless, topics from the Mahāyāna are also touched on, especially in chapters 1, 6 et 9: the eight consciousnesses, Buddha nature, the three natures... (Brunnhölzl, 2009, p.86-87). The 3rd Karmapa gives more details on these themes in the treatises that are based essentially on the sūtras of the Mahāyāna.

25 The *Treatise on Pointing Out Buddha Nature* and the *Treatise on the Distinction between Consciousness and Wisdom* are cited in the commentary of the *Profound Inner Reality.* It was therefore composed before 1325 and very probably after 1322 (Brunnhölzl 2009, p.86).

26 Sct. *Ratnagotravibhāga* (RGV), also known under the ornamental title of *Uttaratantra* or *Gyü Lama* (tib. *Rgyud bla ma*). See Brunnhölzl 2014, p.93-103.

27 Tib. *rnam shes ye shes 'byed pa'i bstan bcos* (NY).

28 For more details on this date, see Brunnhölzl 2009, note 186 p.420.

29 Sct. *Mahāyānasūtrālaṃkāra.*

30 Sct. *Mahāyānasaṃgraha.*

(5) *Ornament That Explains the Dharmadharmatāvibhāga* (1320): he uses the key ideas of the *Dharmadharmatāvibhāga*. It will be useful to use this text again during the presentation of non-conceptual wisdom.

(6) The commentary of *In Praise of Dharmadhātu*[31] (1326 or 1327): Buddha nature is presented as being the *dharmadhātu*.

The first four texts are considered to be fundamental to the understanding of the views and practices of the Vajrayāna and the Mahāmudrā. Besides, the importance of these texts is verified by the fact that the *Profound Inner Reality, the Treatise on the Distinction between Consciousness and Wisdom*, and the *Treatise on Pointing Out Buddha Nature* have been commented[32]. Another text has also received a commentary and benefits from a great interest even today, the *Aspiration Prayer of Mahāmudrā*[33].

It will be the *Treatise on Pointing Out Buddha Nature* that we will primarily focus on.

Treatise on Pointing Out Buddha Nature

Buddha nature is present in all beings

The 3rd Karmapa Rangjung Dorje claims in his *Treatise on Pointing Out Buddha Nature* that the great majority of beings ignore what they truly are. If they engaged in a process of exploration of their

31 Sct. *Dharmadhātustava*.

32 Dwags rams pa Chos rgyal bstan pa (1449-1524), a disciple of the 7th Karmapa Chos grags rgya mtsho (1454-1506) commented the *Profound Inner Reality* in 1495. Dkon mchog 'bangs/yan lag, the 5th Shamarpa (tib. Zhwa dmar pa; 1525-1583) wrote commentaries on the *Profound Inner Reality,* the *Treatise on Pointing Out Buddha Nature* and the *Treatise on the Distinction between Consciousness and Wisdom*. Si tu Paṇ chen Chos kyi 'byung gnas (1700-1774) commented the *Aspiration Prayer of Mahāmudrā*. 'Jam mgon Kong sprul Blo gros mtha' yas (1813-1899) commented the same texts as the 5th Shamarpa did, and he included the commentary of the latter. Finally, the 15th Karmapa mKha' khyab rdo rje (1871-1922) was then also interested in these three texts, but it seems that he especially took up the work of Jamgön Kongtrul Lodrö Thayé. For more information on these different commentaries, see Schaeffer 1995, p.18-21.

33 Tib. *Nges don phyag rgya chen po'i smon lam*. Other poetic works that are quite short have been composed by Rangjung Dorje. Like the *Aspiration Prayer of Mahāmudrā,* they allow to refine or complete the main texts (Brunnhölzl 2009, p.86).

experience by practicing different meditative exercises to purify the adventitious defilements, another reality would appear. It would reflect what they truly are: *Buddhas*[34]. This reality is accessible, since Buddha nature is present in all beings. The *Supreme*

34 NT, stanza 3. In his commentary, Jamgön Kongtrul Lodrö Thayé explains that Buddha nature is a definitive teaching (sct. neyartha, tib. drang don) and not a provisory one (sct. nītārtha, tib. nges don). Three criteria allow the classification of a teaching as provisory (Ruegg, 1989, p.32; Lopez, 1988, p.55 and note 32 p.69). It needs a motive, which is to say a reason to be taught. Then, a provisory teaching carries a meaning that cannot be understood literally, it points to a deeper meaning that is not directly offered by the given teaching. Finally, it is provisory if it is in contradiction with another teaching from the *Buddha*. The teaching must follow three criteria, and not only one of them, to be qualified as provisory. Buddha nature can be interpreted in a way that follows these three criteria. The reason behind its teaching would be to avoid scaring people with emptiness and bring them towards this teaching thanks to Buddha nature. Then, it points to a deeper meaning of emptiness, Buddha nature cannot be understood literally. Finally, Buddha nature, a self, would be in direct contradiction with emptiness, where everything is empty of self. In the *Laṅkāvatāra Sūtra* for example, it is written that Buddha nature was taught to avoid scaring the audience in case they would be afraid of emptiness (LKV ch. XXVIII, Ruegg 1969, p.402; Ruegg 1973 p.27; Ruegg 1989, p.26-27; Mathes 2008, p.2-3) and to invite them to realize emptiness. By interpreting Buddha nature as provisory, a substantialist interpretation is avoided, and it is not only possible to be in agreement with emptiness, but also to demark oneself from heterodox schools. Indeed, Buddha nature seems at first sight to be very similar to the *ātman* or the *brahman* of the Vedānta for example. However, in our context, Buddha nature does not follow these three criteria. We can already notice that the first criterium is not really determinant, in the sense that all the teachings have a reason to be taught. Here, it is about showing the true nature of consciousness and establishing a foundation for meditative practice. Jamgön Kongtrul Lodrö Thayé comments on stanza 13 by saying that if the "motive" is a reason to classify a teaching as provisory, then the second Turning of the Wheel is also as such, in the sense that its goal is to end self-grasping. Therefore, the criterium of the motive is not discriminatory. Regarding the second criteria, it is true that "Buddha nature" cannot be understood literally (the four paradoxes presented in stanza I.23/22 of the *Supreme Continuum* show this very clearly), but that does not mean that its meaning needs to be sought out in another text. One must only look for its meaning beyond ordinary understanding. Finally, the contradiction between emptiness and Buddha nature is only apparent (see end of the third part "All beings are Buddhas" in our commentary).

Therefore, Buddha nature is not a provisory teaching. It is a definitive teaching that shows the ultimate gnoseological constitution. To conclude on the terms "provisory" and "definitive," other interpretations can also be proposed. Buddha nature could be for example qualified as provisory so that it is not interpreted literally. It is perhaps the reason why Büton (bu ston rin chen grub) declares that Buddha nature is a provisory teaching (See Ruegg 1973, p.122-140). Besides, the meaning of "definitive" can also be understood as what is true, both from the superficial and absolute standpoints. In this case, every Turning of the Wheel is definitive, since it is each time about teachings that allow consciousness to get closer to the absolute. However, the third teaching is the definitive and supreme one, since it designates the complete and perfect awakening (Wangchuk 2005, p.184 ; Mathes 2008, p.42).

Continuum presents it extensively, and the *Treatise on Pointing Out Buddha Nature* offers a summary of it in fifty-one stanzas[35].

Transmission of the *Supreme Continuum* in Tibet

India ignored the *Supreme Continuum during six centuries*[36]. The Tibetan tradition relates that Maitrīpa (986-1063)[37] re-discovered this text in an old stupa and that he receives essential instructions. Maitrīpa especially transmitted this text to Sajjana who had an important role in the introduction of the *Supreme Continuum in Tibet. Indeed, Ngog Loden Sherab*[38] (1059-1109) and Tsen Kawoché[39] (born in 1021) have both traveled to Cashmere from Tibet to study this text with him, and they then taught it and commented it[40]. Due to his scholastic approach, the lineage of Ngog Loden Sherab is called "analytical tradition"[41], or the "tradition that explains the works of Maitreya[42]." As for the lineage of Tsen Kawoché, it is named the "meditative tradition"[43] because of his approach that is more largely based on experience. For example, Tsen Kawoché asked Sajjana to give him the texts from Maitreya with special instructions, because he wanted to prepare to die[44]. Marpa Dopa Chökyi Wangchug also contributed to the diffusion of the *Supreme Continuum in Tibet. It seems that he was an important source for the Kagyü lineage in the transmission of the meditative tradition*[45].

---

35 In his introduction of the commentary of the *Supreme Continuum,* Jamgön Kongtrul Lodrö Thayé indicates that the 3rd Karmapa has also composed a summary of the commentary of the *Supreme Continuum* from Zu Gawa Dorjé (gZu dGa´ ba rdo rje, the translator of Tsen Kawoché), but this text is not available today (Mathes, 2008, p.33). For the translation of the introduction from Jamgön Kongtrul Lodrö Thayé, see Hookham 1991, chapter 11.

36 Mathes 2008 p.1-2, Brunnhölzl 2014 p.82.

37 See Roberts 2014, p. 4 (*The Mind of Mahāmudrā*. Boston: Wisdom Publications).

38 rNgog Blo ldan shes rab.

39 bTsan Kha bo che.

40 Brunnhölzl 2014, p.85-87.

41 Tib. *mtshan nyid lugs*.

42 Tib. *byams chos bshad lugs*.

43 Tib. *sgom lugs*.

44 Ruegg, 1969, p.36; Mathes, 2008, p.32-33.

45 Brunnhölzl 2014, p.90. On the link between meditative traditions and the 3rd Karmapa, also see Mathes 2008, p.32-33.

Mahāmudrā and Buddha Nature

The Mahāmudrā of the essence is a teaching that is characteristic of the Kagyüpa lineage, especially stemming from Maitrīpa[46]. It is a meditative practice that "leads to the sudden or instantaneous realization of the natural mind (tha mal gyi shes pa). It requires a realized master who bestows a particular type of blessing called the empowerment of vajra wisdom on a receptive and qualified disciple[47]". The master gives essential instructions[48] in order for the practitioner to be mentally disengaged and realize the luminous nature of the mind[49].

Gampopa (1079–1153) declared that the reference text of the Mahāmudrā is the *Supreme Continuum*[50]. In his Treatise, Rangjung Dorje seems to take up this claim. Different elements show that he undertook the task to re-unite this teaching with the one on Buddha Nature, by considering for example *dharmadhātu and natural consciousness*[51] as synonymous in stanza 13. In this same stanza, the 3rd Karmapa writes that "Noble beings do not improve it, Ordinary beings do not deteriorate it[52]". This excerpt can be assimilated at stanza 154 of the

46 The Mahāmudrā can resort to means derived from the tantras (visualization of deities, recitation of *mantras*, etc.), in which case it is the Mahāmudrā of mantras ; but it can also resort to means that do not stem from the tantras. It is then the Mahāmudrā of essence and the sūtras. This tripartite presentation is clearly marked for the first time by Jamgön Kongtrul Lodrö Thayé during the 19th century, and it is not accepted by all the kagyüpas (Mathes 2006, introduction, 2008 p.44 ; Brunnhölzl 2014, p.151 et s.). In the *Treatise on Pointing Out Buddha Nature,* the perspective that is adopted is the one of the Mahāyāna, therefore, the Mahāmudrā of mantras will not be covered. Besides, the practice of the Mahāmudrā not being relevant to the field of tantras generated polemics. On this topic, see David Jackson, *Enlightenment by a Single Means,* Vienna : Verlag der Österreichischen Akademie der Wissenschaften, 1994 ; Mala 1985, p.402 ; Arguillère 2007, p.444-466 ; and the works of Klaus-Dieter Mathes, notably «Can Sūtra-Mahāmudrā be justified on the Basis of Maitrīpa's Apratiṣṭhānavāda?" In: Pramāṇakīrtiḥ. Papers dedicated to Ernst Steinkellner on the occasion of his 70th birthday. Ed. by B. Kellner, H. Krasser, H. Lasic, M.T. Much, H. Tauscher (Wiener Studien zur Tibetologie und Buddhismuskunde, vol. 70, no. 2), Vienna: Arbeitskreis für tibetische und buddhistische Studien, 545-566, 2007b.

47 Mathes 2008, p. 44.

48 Tib. *man ngag*.

49 The other meaning of *amanasikāra* according to Maitrīpa: a=anutpāda=śūnyatā=luminosité ; manasikāra=svādhiṣṭhāna (self-empowerment), see Mathes 2015.

50 Mathes 2008, p.163; Brunnhölzl 2014, p.152.

51 Mathes, 2008, p.34-45. *Aspiration Prayer of Mahāmudrā* also show the link (Brunnhölzl 2009, note 191, p.421).

52 NT, Stanza 13.

Supreme Continuum, considered as characteristic of the Mahāmudrā: "There is absolutely nothing to remove, Neither anything to add."[53]." Besides, in his commentary of the *Dharmadhātustava, prajñāpāramitā, mahāmudrā and dharmadhātu* are on an equal footing[54].

Additionally, the style in which the *Treatise on Pointing Out Buddha Nature* is written allows a meditative dimension to show through at the side of the theoretical presentation, and invite one to see directly the nature of consciousness[55]. This "experiential" or direct approach can be found for example in stanzas 18 and 19, where stanza 154 of the *Supreme Continuum* is, this time, cited literally. This direct style can also be found when the 3rd Karmapa makes a reference to theses of the Yogācāra and the Madhyamaka[56] (stanzas 11, 12, 18). The commentary of Jamgön Kongtrul Lodrö Thayé sometimes takes up this style (NTC stance 19), but much more discreetly.

Thus, "Buddha nature" and "Mahāmudrā" are major themes of the *Treatise on Pointing Out Buddha Nature*, and the approach is mainly based of of the Mahāyāna standpoint. The 3rd Karmapa also uses references extracted from the *Niruttarayogatantra*, thus indicating that the meaning of Buddha nature is the same both in the sūtras and tantras. This reading hypothesis is confirmed in the *Profound Inner Reality*, a text that is essentially turned towards the tantras, in which Rangjung Dorje describes the same functioning of consciousness as the one exposed in the *Treatise on Pointing Out Buddha Nature* or the *Treatise on the Distinction between Consciousness and Wisdom*[57].

---

53 NT, Stanza 19 [91-92]; RGV, I.154/133. In *The Treasury of Knowledge*, Jamgön Kongtrul Lodrö Thayé associates this passage from the *Supreme Continuum* with the Mahāmudrā of sūtras, see Brunnhölzl 2014, p.152-153. The content that the 3rd Karmapa uses in stanza 19 has also been covered by Maitrīpa or even Vajrapāṇi (Brunnhölzl 2014, p.177 and following). Finally, numerous Indian and Tibetan comments regarding stanza I.154 have been gathered in Annex 3 of *When the clouds part* (Brunnhölzl 2014, p.901-942), thus showing the great interest of this passage and the diverse interpretations that are possible.

54 Mathes, 2008, p.4; Brunnhölzl 2014, p.202. Jamgon Kongtrul Lodrö Thayé also offers another reference to show the link between Mahāmudrā and Buddha nature (Brunnhölzl 2014, p154).

55 This approach combining both "theory and practice" can be also found in other texts of the 3rd Karmapa (Brunnhölzl 2014, p.203-205).

56 According to the 3rd Karmapa, these two currents are not contradictory but complementary. He is not the first one to claim it, and other authors will follow his lead after him (Brunnhölzl 2009, p. 85; 92-94).

57 Brunnhölzl 2009, p. 87.

Context

Thus, the *Treatise on Pointing Out Buddha Nature* is not a text seeking to demonstrate the presence of Buddha nature thanks to several reasonings or proofs[58]. Even if the 3rd Karmapa resorts to different streams of Buddhism, he does not use them to debate or claim the superiority of this or that view[59]. He only offers the essential with a living and direct style, and through this approach, the 3rd Karmapa Rangjung Dorje demarcates himself from the authors that preceded him and will succeed to him. This treatise seems to be first and foremost a memory aid for meditation.

From the 11th century, Tibet experienced a period of high rationalization of the Buddha's thought, which greatly influenced later scholastics. This period "ended up being characterized by the study of the main Indian Buddhist philosophers – primarily Nāgārjuna, Asaṅga and Dignāga as well as their commentators Candrakīrti, Vasubandhu and Dharmakīrti – and by a rigorous adhesion to the

58 He does not even mention the three reasons proving or showing the presence of Buddha nature cited in the *Supreme Continuum*: "All incarnated beings constantly possess the heart of Buddhas because: The perfect kāya of the Buddha radiates; Reality is without separation; The familial lineage [of the Buddha] is present [in all beings],"our translation, Chenique p.98, RGV, I.28/26 (*rdzogs sangs sku ni phro phyir dang/ de bzhin nyid dbyer med phyir dang/ rigs yod phyir na lus can kun/ rtag tu sangs rgyas snying po can/*). In the Tibetan version of the *Supreme Continuum,* the following stanza takes up these three reasons: "It is said that all the wandering beings have the heart of *Buddhas* for three reasons: The wisdom of *Buddhas* is present in all ordinary beings; the undefiled suchness is non-dual; [Beings] are designated [metonymically] by the fruit, [as belonging to] the familial lineage of *Buddhas,*" our translation, Chenique p.98, RGV, I.27/27, (*sangs rgyas ye shes sems can tshogs zhugs phyir/ rang bzhin dri med de ni gnyis med de/ sangs rgyas rigs la de 'bras nyer brtags phyir/ 'gro kun sangs rgyas snying po can du gsungs*). Mipham calls these reasonings "the reasoning in dependance" (tib. *ltos pa'i rigs pa*), "the reasoning of the *dharmatā*" (tib. *chos nyid kyi rigs pa*) and "the reasoning of efficiency" (tib. *bya ba byed pa'i rigs pa*), see Kapstein 1988, p.155-157 and Duckworth 2009, p.120. These three reasons do not really fulfill their function of reasoning, in the sense that they do not provide a real proof of the presence of Buddha nature. Indeed, they assume the possibility and the existence of awakening, and therefore address a reader who already adheres to a certain conception of consciousness's possibility. It is also interesting to note that the 8th Karmapa writes that it is not possible to prove the existence of Buddha nature (see Brunnhölzl 2004 ; 2007, p. 97-99 ; 2009, note 535).

59 On the usage of different doctrines (sct. *siddhānta*, tib. *grub mtha'*, ang. *tenet*), see Kapstein 2000, p.107 and following; Pierre-Julien Harter, *Doxography and philosophy: the usage and significance of school denominations in Red mda' ba Gzhon nu blo gros' ornament of the proofs of consciousness*, University of Chicago.

canons of argumentation and a precise and elegant use of language."[60] The predecessor of the 3rd Karmapa, Karma Pakshi, as for him supported the idea of abandoning philosophical views to attain awakening[61]. Rangjung Dorje also clearly shows the limits of ordinary reason[62], but he nevertheless devotes himself to establishing a coherent philosophical view based on the meditative practice specific to his lineage. He was not the only one to be interested in these topics at his time[63] :

> The XIVth century witnessed an increased interest about subjects associated with the "third cycle of the doctrine": Buddha nature or the "matrix of the tathagata" (*tathāgatagarbha*), the "substrate-consciousness" (*ālayavijñāna*[64]) and the "luminosity of the mind" (*cittaprabhāsa*[65]) in particular. The efforts to satisfactorily give an account of these notions and other related themes, partially acquired their momentum from the diffusion of contemplative and yogic techniques in which similar concepts from other contexts were used. The presence of the same terminology in certain branches of Indian scholastic literature and certain *sutrā* led many scholars to support that the highest teachings of the Buddha could be found in such texts. The debates that followed ended up becoming some of the most ardently disputed Tibetan

60 Our translation, « [Elle] en vint à être caractérisée par l'étude des principaux philosophes bouddhistes indiens — avant tout Nāgārjuna, Asaṅga et Dignāga ainsi que leurs commentateurs Candrakīrti, Vasubandhu et Dharmakīrti — et par une adhésion rigoureuse aux canons de l'argumentation et à un usage précis et élégant du langage », Pol-Droit 2009, p. 338-339.

61 He also wrote the opuscules of philosophical interests. Nonetheless, *The Boundless Ocean* (tib. *Rgya mtsho mtha' yas skor*) is considered as a work that is characteristic of his thought in which a very markedly skeptic mind reveals itself (Kapstein 2000, p. 100 et s.; Pol-Droit 2009, text 11 p.411-414).

62 NT, stanza 12.

63 Establishing a link between natural reason and principial knowledge or wisdom is a recurring problem in the Tibetan tradition (Kapstein 2000, p.97).

64 For a detailed explanation of the *ālayavijñāna*, see Schmithausen Lambert, *Ālaya-vijñāna: On the Origin and the Early Development of a Central Concept of Yogācāra*, International Institute for Buddhist Studies, 1987; Waldron William S., *The Buddhist unconscious,* New York: Routledge Curzon, 2003.

65 The correct term is *cittasya prabhāsvaratā* (remark from K.D. Mathes).

> Buddhist thoughts and are among the richest ones in their ability to open up new perspectives[66]. Pol-Droit 2009, p.339-340.

Rangjung Dorje had a great influence in this regard, and we can also cite Dölpopa Sherab Gyeltsen[67] (1292-1361) or even Longchenpa[68]. Even if they cover similar subjects, the style of the 3rd Karmapa remains uncommon, as well as the philosophical view that he offers[69].

---

66 Our translation, « Le XIVe siècle fut témoin d'un intérêt accru se portant vers des sujets associés au « troisième cycle de la doctrine » : la nature de buddha ou la « matrice des tathāgata » (tathāgatagarbha), la « conscience-substrat » (ālayavijñāna) et la « luminosité de l'esprit » (cittaprabhāsa) notamment. Les efforts pour rendre compte d'une manière satisfaisante de ces notions et d'autres thèmes connexes reçurent en partie leur impulsion de la diffusion de techniques contemplatives et yogiques où il était fait usage de concepts similaires dans d'autres contextes. La présence de la même terminologie dans certaines branches de la littérature scolastique indienne et dans certains sūtra amena quantité de savants à soutenir que les enseignements les plus élevés du Buddha se trouvaient dans de tels textes. Les débats qui en procédèrent finirent par devenir les plus ardemment disputés de la pensée bouddhique tibétaine et sont parmi les plus riches quant au champ des perspectives ouvertes ». Pol-Droit 2009, p.339-340.

67 Dol po pa Shes rab rgyal mtshan. On the eventual encounter between the 3rd Karmapa and Dolpopa, see Schaeffer 1995, p.27 (ch.3); Stearns 1999.

68 Other authors are also presented by K.D. Mathes (Mathes 2008, p.49-129).

69 Buddha nature has not been interpreted in the same way by every author. D.S. Ruegg began to study the Gelugpa texts (Ruegg 1969), and then appeared studies on the interpretation of Buddha nature from other lineages of Tibetan Buddhism (among others: Ruegg 1963; Hookham, S.K., 1991; Stearns 1999, Wangchuk 2005; Mathes 2008; Duckworth 2009). K. Schaeffer and K. Brunnhölzl were specifically interested by the work of the 3rd Karmapa Rangjung Dorje (Schaeffer 1995, Brunnhölzl 2007 et 2009), and in *A direct path to the buddha within* (Mathes 2008), a long section is also dedicated to him. It must be noted that the 3rd Karmapa appears in other works, but only at the margin, or with a specific questioning. Certain studies have notably emphasized that he was shentongpa and that he would even have influenced Dolpopa. However, the 3rd Karmapa has a priori never used that term (Burchardi 2011, p.323), and several types of "shentong" exist. See Schaeffer 1995, p.25-36 ; C. Stearns 1999 Chapter Two "A Historical Survey of the Zhentong Tradition in Tibet," pp.41-45 ; Wangchuk 2005 ; Arguillère 2007, p.285-288 ; Mathes 2008, p.54-56 ; Brunnhölzl 2009, p.95-109 and p.114-117; Burchardi 2011 ; Mathes 2012. Affinities with Longchenpa seem however numerous at the doctrinal level, but Longchenpa developed his philosophical arguments more (Arguillère 2007, p.53 and following).

Translation of the *Treatise on Pointing Out Buddha Nature* from the 3rd Karmapa Rangjung Dorje

A couple of preliminary remarks regarding the translation of the text:

- The translation is based on the texts mentioned in the bibliography[70] as well as the critique edition proposed by K. Schaeffer[71].
- The root text of the 3rd Karmapa is composed of the title, a homage, and fifty-one stanzas, 229 verses in total.
- For the references of the *Supreme Continuum*, we will indicate both the number of the stanzas according to the Johnston edition and according to the commentary from Jamgön Kongtrül Lodrö Thayé.
- The wylie transliteration is used to go from Tibetan characters to the Latin alphabet.

---

70 *Treatise on Pointing Out Buddha Nature – Table of content, de bzhin gshegs pa'i snying po bstan pa'i sa bcad*, in gsung 'bum/ Collected works, vol. 7 (ja) p. 277-281.
Treatise on Pointing Out Buddha Nature, de bzhin gshegs pa'i snying po bstan pa zhes bya ba'i bstan bcos, in gsung 'bum/ Collected works, vol. 7 (ja) p. 282-290.
Commentary of Treatise on Pointing Out Buddha Nature, de bzhin gshegs pa'i snying po bstan pa'i bstan bcos kyi rnam 'grel rang byung dgongs gsal, in mdo sngags mtshams sbyor, vol. 1 p. 420 – 470.

71 Schaeffer 1995, p.93-131. He also cites the different available editions of this text p.21-23.

After citing the *Abhidharma sūtra* and the *Hevajra Tantra*, the 3rd Karmapa explains the key terms of the first citation. In a second part, he presents the main characteristics of ordinary consciousness – which is to say the consciousness that is within *saṃsāra*. The rest of the text is focused on the description of Buddhahood.

Treatise on Pointing Out Buddha Nature[72]

I pay homage to all *Buddhas* and *bodhisattvas*[73]

Although without beginning, it has an end[74].
Naturally pure and consistent with permanent qualities
It is unseen because it has been obscured by a beginningless cocoon [of adventitious defilements]
Like a statue covered in gold[75]. Stanza 1 [1-4]

The *dhātu* of time without beginning
Is the site of all the *dharmas*[76].
Through its presence, all the samsaric existences
And the *nirvāṇa* also, [can] be obtained. Stanza 2 [5-8].

72 Or : *Treatise called demonstration of Buddha Nature.*

73 This homage to the *Buddhas* and *bodhisattvas* shows that this treatise belongs to the categories of the sūtras (Brunnhölzl 2009, note 495).

74 From the standpoint of the superficial truth, it is often claimed that the *saṃsāra* exists since the beginning of times without beginning. It has existed forever. Despite this, it is possible to bring it to an end. It can seem strange to speak of the end of *saṃsāra*, since it is often indicated that *saṃsāra* is endless. However, this is about the end of *saṃsāra* at an individual level. There will always be beings who suffer, but that does not mean that the end of *saṃsāra* is not possible within one particular consciousness. It is also possible to understand "without beginning" from the standpoint of absolute truth, as suggested by Stanza 4 of the *Treatise on Pointing Out Buddha Nature.*

75 This stanza is attributed to the *Abhidharmasūtra* according to the 5th Shamarpa and Kongtrul. As for Takasaki, he writes that the source is unknown (Takasaki 1966, p.224). See also Brunnhölzl 2009, note 500.

76 The *dharmas* designate the phenomena and qualities of a Buddha (*buddhadharma*) – « See *Samādhirājasūtra* XXXII.8ab (SRS 19524), where phenomena (*dharmas*) are in reality buddha qualities (*buddhadharmas*): "All dharmas are buddha-dharmas [for those] who are trained in *dharmatā.*" (*sarvadharmā buddhadharmā dharmatāyāṃ ya* śikṣitāḥ). Note that *ya* is used for *ye* or the like for metrical reasons", Remark from K.D.Mathes.

Ordinary beings are nothing else than *Buddhas*
But they are obscured with adventitious defilements.
If they are purified, that is Buddhahood.
This has been written in a tantra. *Hevajra Tantra,* 2nd Part, IV.69, Stanza 3 [9-12].

It has been declared in [the *Abhidharmasūtra*]: "without beginning"
Consequently, absolutely nothing exists beforehand.
Time is this one instant,
It does not come from another place. Stanza 4 [13-16].

The *dhātu* is without creator
But because of its specific characteristics, it is expressed as such. Stanza 5 [17-18]

Phenomena are explained as being appearances
Of *saṃsāra* but also *nirvāṇa,*
This is named "the ground of ignorance's tendencies[77]."
Authentic or non-authentic thoughts,
The movement of mental formations is the cause which [phenomena] are born from.
This causal condition is explained as being the *ālaya*. Stanza 6 [19-24].

---

77 "This term, found in both the Śrīmālādevīsūtra and the Uttaratantra (I.138 and III.34), is an equivalent of the ālaya, remainders of which are even present in arhathood (personal nirvāṇa) and on the ten bhūmis of bodhisattvas," Brunnhölzl 2009, note 515). "In the *Ratnagotravibhāga*, the bag chags kyi sa is the first of four obstacles to the attainment of the four perfections. The obstacles are : condition, cause, origination, and destruction: RGVV p. 32, l. 17: "Of these, the defining characteristic of condition is the level of the imprints of ignorance just as [ordinary] ignorance for intentional deeds. The defining characteristic of cause is undefiled action which has the level of the imprints of ignorance as condition, just like intentional deeds."", Remark from K.D.Mathes.

The site is the heart of victorious ones.
Non authentic imagination
Remains entirely within the purity of the [nature of] consciousness. Stanza 7 [25-27].

This purity itself is now present[78].
Despite its presence, we do not perceive it
Because of ignorant imagination
It is the *saṃsāra*[79]. Stanza 8 [28-30].

If this in itself is purified, *nirvāṇa* manifests itself.
It is conventionally[80] designated as the end. Stanza 9 [31-32].

Beginning and end rest on nothing else than imagination.
By mental formations, comparable to the wind
Karma and afflictions are produced
By [mental formations], *skandhas, dhātus* and āyatanas,[81]
All phenomena that appear in a dual form are manifested. Stanza 10 [33-37].

The one who adopts and rejects [these imaginary objects] is in illusion.

---

78 "Lines 25–28 echo Madhyāntavibhāga I.1," Brunnhölzl 2009, note 517.

79 "Lines 29–30 echo Dharmadharmatāvibhāga lines 24–27 and Mahāyānasūtrālaṃkāra VI.4cd," Brunnhölzl 2009, note 518.

80 Tib. *tha snyad*: "Designates, in a narrow sense, a purely verbal, *terminological* convention, but in a wider sense, can be said of what is considered as such or such, without any other foundation than usage, habit. In the particular context of the madhyamaka, it does not necessarily seem to be a convention with a social, collective nature – we can absolutely talk of some sort of "individual convention" in the case, for example, of the madman's hallucinations or even simply the appearances of a dream. Therein, the term of "convention" is perhaps not ideal to describe what is at stake. Synonym of "surface" or "superficial."" Arguillère 2008, p.212.

81 In the Abhidharma, these are the categories in which the different elements of reality are classified. *Skandha* can be translated by "aggregate," *dhātu* by "elements" and *āyatana* by "sources of perception."

By rejecting our own appearances, where will they cease?
By adopting our own appearances, what appears?
Isn't dualistic grasping misleading? Stanza 11 [38-41].

Understanding this is taught as antidote.
Yet, this understanding of non-duality is not the truth.
Otherwise, the thought of non-existence would become [an even grosser] thought.
[If] you understand emptiness as the analysis in different parts of form, etc.
Aren't you misleading yourself?
Yet, this is taught in order to stop the grasping onto truths. Stanza 12 [42-47].

All [phenomena] are neither true nor delusive.
Scholars claim that they are comparable to the [reflection of] the moon on water[82].
This natural consciousness is called *dharmadhātu*[83] or heart of the victorious.
Noble beings do not improve it
Ordinary beings do not deteriorate it.
Although it is unavoidably expressed with different conventional terms,
Its meaning is not understood through expressions. Stanza 13 [48-55].

The incessant manifestation[84] [of the heart]

82 "Lines 48–49 summarize *Yuktiṣaṣṭikā* (*Sixty Stanzas of Reasoning*), verse 45," Brunnhölzl 2009, note 531.

83 On the identity between "*dharmadhātu*" and "*tathāgatagarbha*," also see Takasaki 1966, p.197-198.

84 Sct. *lalita*, tib. *rol ba*. S. Arguillère translates this term by "entertainment," "with the double meaning of "play" and "becoming diverses, multiplying." Comp. Fr. Chenet, *Psychogenèse et cosmogonie dans le Yoga-vāsiṣṭha*, t. 2, pp. 622 *sq.* » (Arguillère 2007, p.214). *Rol pa* is a terminology specific to Dzogchen.

Through its sixty-four qualities
Is only an approximation. Each of them
[Possesses] tens of millions of them. Stanza 14 [56-59].

Knowing what is appropriate and what is not,
Karmic maturations,
Knowing the dispositions, faculties, and aspirations of all wandering beings,
The paths, the *dhyānas*, [having] the divine eye,
Remembering the places of rebirth and [being] at peace.
These are the ten strengths. Stanza 15 [60-64][85].

The four wisdoms of self-confidence[86] rest upon these [ten strenghts]:
Being awakened to all phenomena,
Teaching the obstacles, the path and the cessation.
No one can put them into question[87]. Stanza 16 [65-67].

This is the cause of the eighteen [distinctive qualities],
(1) Absence of confusion, (2) Absence of futile speech,
(3) Unshakeable vigilance (4) Constant meditative balance,
(5) Not having diverse denominations (6) Absence of indifference without examination
(7) Motivation, (8) Perseverance, (9) Rememoration,
(10) *Samādhi,* (11) Superior Knowledge
(12) An unshakeable wisdom that sees full liberation,
(13-15) All the actions are preceded by wisdom,

85 This stanza cites the *Supreme Continuum* (RGV III.5-6).

86 "The Sanskrit term vaiśāradya (translated as "fearlessness" into Tibetan) literally means self-confidence (also skill, expertise, wisdom, infallibility)," Brunnhölzl 2009, note 542.

87 This stanza points to the *Supreme Continuum* (RGV III.8). The four wisdoms of self-confidence are compared to the intrepidity of the lion.

(16-18) Absence of obscurations towards the three times.

The *dharmakāya* possesses [these] thirty-two [qualities] [88]. Stanza 17 [68-77].

Currently, we are going in the opposite direction of [these qualities].

Because we are not certain of what is, just as it is

We produce an imaginary world that thinks existing beings, which [actually] do not exist.

These thoughts that are born from these [objects which are considered as existing] is the dependent nature.

Not [re]cognizing the nature that is perfectly established[89], we get stuck in our own activity. Alas!

Those who realize what is true, these qualities of the *dharmakāya*

Know reality.

[Even] their actual weak presence is true.

Through the rejection of this knowledge, we fabricate what is not real

And we follow [the illusory appearances], agitated like waves. Stanza 18 [78-88].

Understand what is, just as it is,

And you will obtain the powers of that.

---

88 This stanza points to the *Supreme Continuum* (RGV III.11-13).

89 "In Idealism, (skt. *Vijñānavāda*), simple duality of the absolute and the superficial is found entirely re-elaborated through the device of the *triple nature,"* Arguillère 2002, p.8. The 3rd Karmapa also mentions the three natures but only once in the *Treatise on Pointing Out Buddha Nature* in Stanza 18. He gives more detailed explanations in his commentary of the *Distinction between dharma and dharmatā.* Considering the multiplicity of interpretations of these three natures among the authors, and sometimes even within the same piece of work (it is for example the case with Longchenpa, see Arguillère 2007, p.254-284), we will not cover this topic here since we have few elements to our disposition in the text. "It is unfortunate that neither Rang byung nor any of his commentators provides a source for this doctrine," Schaeffer 1995, note 37 p.99. On the different interpretations of these three natures, see Schaeffer 1995, note 24 p.49; Mathes 2000; Brunnhölzl 2007, p.60-62.

There is absolutely nothing to remove
Neither anything to add.
What is real must be seen correctly
The one who truly *sees*[90] is liberated
The *dhātu* is empty from adventitious defilements
That are characterized by being separable from them.
But it is not empty of its supreme qualities
That are characterized by being inseparable from them. Stanza 19 [89-98][91].

The nature of these two *rūpakāyas* [born] from this [*dharmakāya*],
[Consists in] thirty-two major marks and [eighty] minor marks. Stanza 20 [99-100].

[The cause of] the obtention of the qualities is the body itself,
This body is not created by a self, such as Cha, Iśvara
Or Brahmā, neither by external atoms [that are really] existing
Nor by dissimulated [objects].
When the five impure doors, because of dualistic grasping, are refined,
At this moment, we conventionally say that there is obtention [of the qualities]. Stanza 21 [101-107].

Thus, *nāḍī, vāyu,* and *tilaka,*
[When they become] pure, are the pure *rūpakāya.*

---

90 The verbs "lta ba" and "mthong ba" mean "to see." But the first designates the dual view and the second designates the non-dual view. In order to mark this difference, non-dual view is indicated in italics.

91 NT, Stanza 19, [91-94]: the 3rd Karmapa uses an important passage of the *Supreme Continuum* (RGV, I. 154-155/ 133-134 ; Brunnhölzl, 2014 note 1488 p.1103).

Non-purified, they are the impure *rūpakāya.* Stanza 22 [108-110].

[Let's take the example] of a beryl covered with stains
Whose qualities, consequently, cannot appear.
By purifying it with an alkaline solution and woven cloth,
[Then], with an acidic solution and a wool fabric,
[Finally] with pure water and [fine cotton] from Kāśī
Through this purification, the beryl is a jewel source of accomplishment of all wishes. Stanza 23 [111-116].

Consciousness is like beryl.
To purify it from its three stains -
[Obscurations] of afflictions, knowledge and absorptive meditation -,
One must completely train on the paths of accumulation, unification
On the seven impure bhūmis and the three pure bhūmis. Stanza 24 [117-121].

When the imagination that is non authentic
Meets the imagination that is authentic
Imagination is freed up, just as two wooden sticks burn [when rubbed against one another].
The grasping of the four characteristics
What is to be abandoned, the remedies, suchness, and realization
Is liberated. Stanza 25 [122-126].

At this one moment, the flowers of marks bloom
Within those who are endowed with a space-body.
Impure, impure and pure, completely pure
Express three phases

Ordinary beings, *bodhisattvas* and the *Buddhas* respectively[92].

But Buddhahood is not a new development,

It is identical before and after

The heart of *Buddhas* is immutable[93]

"Change" expresses [only] the liberation of impurities[94]. Stanza 26 [127-136].

Those who place [their consciousness] within inferior views,

Think that the qualities of a *Buddha* are without cause,

Or that they are not within us but produced

By external causes and conditions.

How is that different from the eternalist and nihilist standpoints? Stanza 27 [137-141].

The mental formations [of a *Buddha*] appear [as] birthing and disappearing momentarily

Similar to impure mental formations.

If it was not that way,

The activity of the *rūpakāyas* would be interrupted.

Yet, we do not express it through the name of "mental formation,"

But by "discriminating wisdom." Stanza 28 [142-147].

The nature of the great elements etc., is grasped [by ordinary beings]

And reveal their powerful essence.

Whether it is [from the standpoint] of illusion or absence of illusion,

---

92 Lines 129-132 correspond to RGV I.147.

93 Lines 134-135 correspond to RGV I.51cd and resemble *The Ornament of the Mahāyāna Sūtras* (IX.22ac).

94 On the different interpretations of "*gnas 'gyur*," see Higgins 2012, p.141-143.

There is absolutely no difference at the level of appearance.
Stanza 29 [148-151].

The difference is the presence or not of dualistic grasping.
If it was not the case,
How could the activity of the victorious ones be in relationship [with the world]? Stanza 30 [152-154].

[Awakened activity] is expressed through the example of the jewel that fulfills all wishes
It explains the manifestation of the power of the absence of thoughts.
But... Stanza 31 [155-156].

... it is not only [an appearance of the] continuum [of consciousness] of others
If it is the case, others' continuum of consciousness would become wisdom
By claiming this, wisdom becomes illusion. Stanza 32 [157-159].

"[Wisdom] grasps onto its own appearances"
If this is claimed, then a mirror would grasp onto
And conceptualize its appearances also. Stanza 33 [160-162].

Although diverse illusionary [appearances] of ordinary beings
Appear like objects to wisdom
Wisdom is not affected by the illusion.
For example, amidst space
Appear the great elements that are born and cease
But these births and cessations do not affect space. Stanza 34 [163-168][95].

95 Lines 166-168 summarize the *Supreme Continuum* (I. 53-57/50-53 et 62/56).

Similarly, although the wisdom of the victorious ones enters in relationship with beings

It is not affected.

Having said that, it is not named "illusion"

But "all accomplishing wisdom." Stanza 35 [169-172].

[When] the three veils purify themselves, the mental resting [on the foundation of everything]

[Becomes wisdom] of everything, [supreme] peace.

Thanks to their love and great compassion,

The *saṃbhogakāya* and others appear to those [that are to be guided].

This is expressed in order to refute certain people [thinking that]

The moment of obtention of Buddhahood is equivalent [to the fruit] of the Hīnayāna. Stanza 36 [173-178].

Wisdom is permanent in three [ways].

Permanence of nature is the *dharmakāya.*

Through continuity, permanence is the *saṃbhogakāya.*

[Permanence of] uninterrupted continuity is the *nirmāṇakāya.* Stanza 37 [179-182][96].

There are three impermanent [phenomena]

Emptiness that is mentally created is impermanent.

The moving conceptual mental is impermanent.

The six conditioned consciousnesses are impermanent. Stanza 38 [183-186].

---

96 Lines180-182 correspond to *Mahāyānasūtrālaṃkāra,* IX.66cd. The *dharmakāya* is permanent because it does not depend on the causes and conditions. The *sambhogakāya* is permanent in terms of continuity, the teaching of the dharma is continually taught to people that are able to receive it. As for *nirmāṇakāya*, it is permanent in the sense that a form is always available to incarnate awakening.

However, the three permanent wisdoms are present within themselves.

The three impermanent ones are the impurities

The three permanent ones are the wisdoms. Stanza 39 [187-189].

[The *dharmadhātu*] is not similar to the self of non-Buddhists

Because [the self of non-Buddhists] is a mental imputation whereas [the *dharmadhātu*] is not[97]. Stanza 40 [190-191].

[Awakening] is not similar to the peace of the *śrāvakas* and the *pratyekabouddhas*

---

97 Buddha Nature could be assimilated to a teaching on the self (sct. *ātman*, tib. *bdag*) of non-Buddhist schools (sct. *tīrthikas*). It is especially the position of the branch of "Critical Buddhism" (on this topic, see *Pruning the Bodhi tree, The storm above critical buddhism*, edited by Jamie Hubbard and Paul L. Swanson, University of Hawaï press, 1997; Zimmerman 2002 p.82-84). The term "*tīrthika*" designates all the traditions that are not in agreement with Buddhism. Therefore, this pertains to many philosophical and religious schools and Rangjoung Dorje does not give us more information on the doctrines that he aims at. Differentiating Buddhism as it is presented by the 3rd Karmapa from these traditions cannot be executed in the context of this study. To do this, we would have to explain in detail each one of the views considered as heterodox, study whether their interpretation of the Self is the same as in the *Treatise On Pointing Out Buddha Nature* and whether the experience which it points to is different or not. Indeed, even if the terms used to designate this self are identical to these used by the non-Buddhists, this does not mean that the experience which they point to is identical. Only the term "mental imputation" (tib. *yid kyis btags*) is given to distinguish the non-Buddhist Self of the *dharmakāya*. In the *Vocabulaire du bouddhisme,* "imputation" is defined as having the characteristic of inefficient fiction (Arguillère 2002, p.59). How could a Self be an inefficient fiction? This could correspond to an explanation or understanding of the self in which emptiness would not have been included. At a theoretical level, an author can elaborate a thought of the self without deconstructing the ordinary self or by deconstructing it completely. At a practical level, which is to say meditative, imputing a self would come down to wanting to engage oneself in direct ways, without having performed the preliminary steps necessary to an authentic meditation on the nature of consciousness. As such, even if the term "*tīrthika*" designates the non-Buddhist schools, insisting on the mental imputations would give it another signification. The *tīrthikas* would designate the people who reify the absolute self in one way or another. It would be then completely possible to defend Buddha Nature as it is exposed in the *Treatise on Pointing Out Buddha Nature* and to be a *tīrthika*. For another presentation of the link between Buddha Nature and a Self, see Karl Brunnhölzl, *In Praise of Dharmadhātu* (2007), pp.102-109.

Because it displays all the qualities of formal bodies. Stanza 41 [192-193].

[Formal bodies] are not similar to the body of [ordinary] beings
Because they are not born in contaminated conditions. Stanza 42 [194-195].

[*Buddhas*] do not regress
Because they simultaneously perceive what is and [the how] of what is. Stanza 43 [196-197].

Impurities never emerge again
Because [*Buddhas*] are free from the imagination that differentiates them. Stanza 44 [198-199].

Consequently, this Buddhahood, consciousness itself,
Is present, but we do not know it. Stanza 45 [200-201].

At the moment of realization,
Similar to the appeasing of the warmth of the metal
And ocular illness,
The consciousness and the wisdom of a *Buddha*
Cannot be said to be existing or non-existing[98]. Stanza 46 [202-206].

Since there is ultimately no birth[99],
There is, in reality, no liberation either
Buddhas are like space,
And ordinary beings have the same characteristics.
Since this shore of the *saṃsāra* and the other shore of the

98 *The Ornament of the Mahāyāna Sūtras*, IX, 25.

99 Sct. *Mahāyānaviṃśikā.*

nirvāṇa are without birth
There is no nature of *nirvāṇa* either.
Consequently, composed phenomena are entirely empty
It is the sphere of experience of the omniscient ones' wisdom[100]. Stanza 47 [207-214].

As it is subtle, it is not an object of listening.
As it is absolute, it is not [an object] of reflection.
As the *dharmatā* is deep,
It is not [an object] of mundane meditations and others[101]. Stanza 48 [215-218].

The sphere of experience of wisdom that knows itself [perceives the absolute][102].
The trust that arises by itself gives birth to the absolute[103].

---

100 *Mahāyānaviṃśikā*, Stanzas 2–3.

101 *Supreme Continuum,* II.32/162.

102 This sentence or sentences that are very similar can be found in several texts, sūtras or tantras, from the Madhyamaka or Yogācāra traditions (*Laṅkāvatārasūtra* et *Saṃdhinirmocanasūtra*; *Kāyatrayastotra* of Nāgārjuna; *Prajñāpradīpa* of Bhāvaviveka ; *Prasannapadā* and Madhyamakāvatārabhāṣya of Candrakīrti ; *Dharmadharmatāvibhāgavṛtti* of Vasubandhu; *Uttaratantra* (I.7a, 9b, 17b, 70b, V.1d) and the *Ratnagotravibhāgavyākhya* (for more details, see Brunnhölzl 2009, note 645).

103 sct. *śraddhā*, tib. *dad pa.* See also RGV I.153/132. "Faith" or "trust." At first glance, we could think that trust is reserved only to certain people, it's not available to everyone. The term "trust" can also imply that the rational process is excluded. What is the meaning of this term? Asaṅga explains in his commentary of the *Supreme Continuum* that trust is necessary for inferior people to the advanced bodhisattva (Ruegg, 1969, p.300-301). Jamgön Kongtrül Lodrö Thayé gives more precisions in the commentary of this stanza. At the end of this excerpt, trust "gives birth to wisdom that directly realizes highest wisdom." Jamgön Kongtrul Lodrö Thayé is even clearer in his commentary of stanza I.153 in the *Supreme Continuum,* where he cites again the three types of trust distinguished by Gampopa in his *Dam chos yid bzhin gyi nor but har par in po che'i rgyan zhes bya ba bzhugs* (*Jewel Ornament of Liberation)* – the convinced trust (tib. *yid ches pa'i dad pa*), the desiring trust (tib. *'dod pa'i dad pa*) and the lucid trust (tib. *dang ba'i dad pa*). Convinced trust is the certitude that the teachings of the *Buddha* are true, for example the law of karma, the functioning of the mind, etc. This trust, faith or certitude, is born from study and reflection. The desiring trust consists in the aspiration to practice the path. Being sure of the possibility of liberation, the person dives into the practice. Finally, lucid trust corresponds to the step where the practitioner develops a great trust in the qualities of the three gems associated with joy. Perhaps this trust is close to "mos gus ," devotion (this term can be found in the Kagyü

Alas, as they do not realize the [profound way of being]
Childish beings wander in the ocean of *saṃsāra*. Stanza 49 [219-222].

By the power of the great sage [104],
Of Mañjuśrīghoṣa, Maitreya and Avalokiteśvara,
Rangjoung Dorjé has written [this treatise]. Stanza 50 [223-225].

May all the wandering beings understand this heart of the *Buddhas*
Perfectly and without mistake.
The establishing of the heart of *Buddhas*, quintessence of the diamond vehicle,
Is complete. Stanza 51 [226-229].
Śubhaṃ (auspicious)

lineage, see Mathes 2008, p.189). There is no more doubt, but it is not blind either (tib. *mig med pa'i dad pa*) since consciousness has already passed certain stages beforehand. Thanks to the development of superior knowledge, ordinary consciousness transforms little by little in a lucid trust. Thus, the term "trust" can be applied in different contexts and designate levels of knowledge from the most ordinary to the most absolute one.

104 "Rangjung Dorje's own outline says, "The manner of obtaining the buddha heart from prajñā, love, and compassion" (which are embodied by mañjuśrī, maitreya, and avalokiteśvara, respectively," Brunnhölzl 2009, note 647.

All beings are Buddhas

Introduction

At the beginning of the *Treatise on Pointing Out Buddha Nature*, two citations from the *Abhidharma sūtra* and *tantra Hevajra* summarize the situation of consciousness. First of all, the *Abhidharma sūtra*[105]:

> Although without beginning, it has an end.
> Naturally pure and consistent with permanent qualities
> It is unseen because it has been obscured by a beginningless cocoon [of adventitious defilements]
> Like a statue covered in gold. Stanza 1 [1-4]
>
> The *dhātu* of time without beginning
> Is the site of all the *dharmas*.
> Through its presence, all the samsaric existences
> And the *nirvāṇa* also, [can] be obtained. NT, Stanza 2 [5-8].

This citation indicates that two states of consciousness are possible: *saṃsāra* and *nirvāṇa*. The former characterizes consciousness entrenched in a cocoon of defilement without beginning and the latter points to the realization of dhātu, which is pure and full of

105 Two types of *nirvāṇa* will be distinguished later – "personal" *nirvāṇa* and great *nirvāṇa* or full awakening.

countless permanent qualities. Both samsāra and nirvana are based on dhātu, a consciousness free of defilement. Dhātu is considered the cause of awakening[106] – in other words, its presence guarantees that all beings can reach perfect Buddhahood. The third Karmapa goes back over the example of a covered golden statue to illustrate the two possible states of mind[107].

Then, Rangjung Dorje cites the *Hevajra tantra*, which claims that all beings are Buddhas:

> Ordinary beings are nothing else than *Buddhas*. NT, Stanza 3, [9].

Unlike the *Supreme Continuum* which states that "all beings have Buddha Nature[108]," the Hevajra tantra does not differentiate between ordinary beings and *buddhas*. In the first case, it is possible to think that all beings hold inside a potential similar to a seed which they must develop. In the second case, the identity of both ordinary beings and Buddhas is clear: all buddha qualities are already present[109]. Purifying the veils is all that is needed for them to reveal:

> Ordinary beings are nothing else than *Buddhas*
> But they are obscured with adventitious defilements.
> If they are purified, that is Buddhahood.
> This has been written in a tantra. *Hevajra Tantra*, 2nd Part, IV.69, NT, Stanza 3 [9-12].

---

106 Cf. *Treatise on Pointing Out Buddha Nature,* Stanza 5.

107 Nine examples are presented in the *Supreme Continuum* (I.95/82 et s.). These examples are extracted from the *Tathāgatagarbhasūtra*: a buddha's presence in a decaying lotus; honey amidst bees; a grain in its husk; gold in filth; a treasure underground; a shoot and so on sprouting from a little fruit; a statue of Buddha in a tattered rag, a king's presence in a destitute woman's womb. For every example, the idea is the same: the wrinkled lotus, the bees, the shell, the trash, the soil, the skin of the fruit, the poor pregnant woman, and the mold of soil represent the different veils that cover what we really are; and Buddhahood is represented by honey, the treasure, the king, etc.

108 *gro kun sangs rgyas snying po can*, RGV I.27/ 27.

109 See discussions around the compound name « *tathāgatagarbha* », is it a bahuvrīhi or a tatpuruṣa? Ruegg, 1969, p.507-513; Zimmermann, 2002, p.41-46.

Transforming Experience

The great principles linked to Buddha Nature are simple to understand. Our true nature is covered by different cognitive and emotional veils - studying and applying different meditative techniques is enough to remove them. Thus, by walking the path, one's perception goes from an ordinary state to an awakened state. The nine examples which can be found for instance in the *Supreme Continuum* among other places illustrate these principles very well[110].

However, understanding the meaning of all beings having a Buddha Nature is not easy - how is it possible? Moreover, what is the ordinary perception and the dualistic grasping of the samsāra? What are its characteristics and why should one get rid of them? Because of suffering, the first Truth of Noble beings tells us. But how can we undo their causal link? How does the going from an ordinary vision to an awakened vision work?

Buddha Nature, awakening... many concepts that can appear very abstract, almost surreal. However, different Buddhist texts show with great precision how to progress on the path and also mention the different stages before reaching a complete and perfect awakening. In other words, the terminology regarding awakening, which can seem abstract at first, actually points to different lived experiences – experiences of the self and the world – that are different from that of an ordinary being. We must remember that the *Treatise on Pointing Out Buddha Nature* belongs to the meditative transmission of the *Supreme Continuum*, and is closer to an aide-memoire than a statement seeking to demonstrate at any cost the presence of Buddhahood. We could say that in particular, this text has a practical vocation – it shows us what is to be discovered inside of ourselves in concise ways.

The first question that we will thus try to answer is the following: how does one understand that everything is already here permanently while Buddhahood is not manifest? The *Supreme Continuum* offers three reasons to explain this universal presence, but they do not truly succeed in their demonstrative attempts[111]. Establishing the link between non-awakened and awakened consciousness

110 RGV.I.95/82 et s.

111 RGV I.28/26, see note during the presentation of the text.

is thus not obvious, these two modes of consciousness seem completely different – with love and wisdom on one side, confusion and suffering on the other. Nonetheless, the text constantly claims that they do have a common foundation. The concept of co-emergence[112] is also considered, as a central concept for the practice of Mahāmudrā, which Dakpo Tashi Namgyal defines in the following way:

> « Connate » refers to all phenomena (all animate and inanimate entities) and the dharmatā of each of those (their thusness tathātā) being present simultaneously from the beginning with neither preceding nor following the other. *Moonbeams*, p.268-269[113].

This brings us to our second main question : Buddha Nature is the teaching reference of Mahāmudrā[114], but how is it possible to recognize natural consciousness – that absolute dimension which is present in each instant ? How to understand that "there is absolutely nothing to remove, neither anything to add" ? What does the practitioner have to accomplish, what inner move must they cultivate to see what is?

In order to apprehend these questions, it seems necessary to develop a phenomenological approach of Buddha Nature, not only a conceptual one, in order for one to access the content of one's perception. A descriptive approach to lived experiences could indeed better capture the implications of Buddha Nature : is it a fiction, an unreachable ideal, or an experience within hand's reach? Additionally, complementing the hermeneutic coherence of this text, an experimental coherence could also be shed into light.

Is ineffability an issue ?

The theme of awakening's ineffability has been present since the beginnings of Buddhism. Walpola Rahula compares this experience

112 Tib. *lhan cig tu kyes pa.*

113 Book written by Dakpo Tashi Namgyal. It will be one of our references when meditation is described.

114 See presentation of the text.

as that of a fish. The latter is not able to understand the experience of the turtle, which can be both in water[115] and on solid ground. The 3rd Karmapa also writes that this topic is ineffable – it is above any appellation[116]. The *Supreme Continuum* gives more precisions by indicating the different points that are inconceivable.

> [The buddha element] is pure and yet has affliction.
> [Enlightenment] was not afflicted and yet is purified.
> Qualities are totally indivisible [and yet unapparent].
> [Activity] is spontaneous and yet without any thought.
> *Buddha Nature,* p.23[117].

This verse indicates the main topics linked to Buddha Nature – its presence is pure but accompanied with obscurations – despite its purity, purification is necessary, its qualities are inseparable, and Buddha's actions happen spontaneously without reference point. These four points are the ones to shed light on in order to understand Buddha Nature[118].

> Buddha Nature is even inconceivable for the *bodhisattvas* :
> Buddha element, buddha awakening,
> buddha qualities, and buddha activity
> cannot be thought, not even by purified beings.
> They are the field of experience of their guides. *Buddha Nature, p.73*[119].

115 Walpola Rahula p.35.

116 NT, stanza 13.

117 *Dag dang nyon mongs dang ldan phyir/ kun nas nyon mongs med dag phyir/ rnam par dbye ba med chos phyir/ lhun grub rnam par mi rtogs phyir/*(RGV, I.25/24). All the citations in Tibetan from the *Supreme Continuum* are taken from the book *Le message du futur Bouddha* from François Chenique.

118 D.S. Ruegg works on these questions in Ruegg, 1969, p.297-308.

119 *Sangs rgyas khams dang sangs rgyas byang chub dang/ Sangs rgyas chos dang sangs rgyas phrin las te/ dag pa'i sems can gyis kyang bsam bya min/ 'di ni 'dren pa rnams kyi spyod yul yin/* RGV, V. 1/279.

Only Buddhas can understand Buddha Nature, awakening, Buddhahood's qualities, and awakened activity. This is probably the reason why Rangjung Dorje writes in stanza 49 that the absolute is born from trust, as opposed to listening, reflection, and mundane meditations:

> As it is subtle, it is not an object of listening.
>
> As it is absolute, it is not [an object] of reflection.
>
> As the *dharmatā* is deep,
>
> It is not [an object] of mundane meditations and others.
>
> The sphere of experience of wisdom that knows itself[120] perceives the absolute].
>
> The trust that arises by itself gives birth to the absolute[121].
> NT, Stanza 48-49 [219-220].

These claims lead one to think in the first place that this topic cannot be subjected to discourse, it would be absolutely inaccessible to those who are not awakened or do not trust. Buddha Nature would therefore be more like a presence in which one can trust but not understand. And yet, Buddha Nature is *the topic* to know, it is the heart of theory and practice. Moreover, there was mention since the beginnings of Buddhism that the words of the Buddha must not only be trusted because they are the words of the Buddha – Buddhahood must be found amidst one's experience[122]. Jamgön Kongtrul Lodrö Thayé also indicates the latter:

> Therefore, [Rangjung Dorje] passes on this virtue to all beings, the objects to whom he dedicates it. By the power of that, may all these sentient beings, through perfectly studying, reflecting, and meditating on this profound instruction on the essential point—this very buddha heart that exists in themselves—know[123] and realize[124] the basic nature pure of all adventitious stains without

120 Tib. *Rang rig ye shes*.

121 Cf. RGV I.153/ 132; II. 31-33/ 161-163.

122 See *Kālāma sutta*.

123 Tib. *shes*.

124 Or « see directly » (tib. *rtogs*).

> error! This determination of the buddha heart, which is clearly and extensively taught in the causal yāna, is [also] the quintessence of the view of the vajrayāna of secret mantra. Therefore, this completes the explanation of the final view. NTC Stanza 51, in *Luminous Heart* p.255.

This passage shows that Buddhahood is the important point to understand and the means of reflection are not disqualified, unlike in stanza 49 of the root text. Rangjung Dorje also mentions in some places that it is necessary to conduct a reflection process and develop certitudes about the nature of phenomena[125]. Therefore, even if Rangjung Dorje talks about trust[126] as mean to access the absolute, he does not exclude other faculties that are a priori antinomic with the fruit.

In stanza 49, the 3rd Karmapa uses the term « *rang rig ye shes* » - "wisdom that knows itself[127]." According to Jamgön Kongtrul Lodrö Thayé, this is the abbreviation of « *so sor rang rig pa'i ye shes*[128] .» This term is used in numerous Indian traditions since the pāli[129]

125 See NT Stances 18, 19, 25, but also RGV, V.6/284 ; V.15/290.

126 Different types of trust exist, see note in the root text, NT Stanza 49.

127 David Higgings mentions that *rang rig* is often employed in Dzogchen literature. It is closely associated to other gnoseological terms such as luminosity (tib. *'od gsal*) or Buddha Nature (Higgins 2012, p.86-87). The study of D. Higgins that focus on the philosophical foundations of Dzogchen (Higgins 2012), as well as other works related Longchenpa, such as D. Germano (1992) et S. Arguillère (2007), will be cited several times. Even if the 3rd Karmapa is especially considered as the master of the Kagyü lineage, he also has an in-depth understanding of the Dzogchen (see « a couple of biographical elements » previously discussed; Arguillère 2007, p.50 ; Mathes 2008, p.52). This is why we will allow ourselves to sometimes use a couple of commentaries regarding thoughts from Longchenpa or the Dzogchen to shed light on certain claims from the *Treatise on Pointing Out Buddha Nature*. We hypothesize that this choice is coherent for the mentioned elements, but a more in-depth study would be necessary to be certain of its validity.

128 NTC, Stanza 49.

129 Matthew Kapstein (2000) shows that the use of « *so sor rang rig pa'i ye shes* » is ancient. He questions Paul Williams' interpretation that includes « *so sor rang rig pa'i ye shes* » as « a simple reflexive gnosis », an interpretation that would be specific to the Dzogchen. Additionally, « *rang rig* » or « self-consciousness » has been intensely debated in India and Tibet. For a review of these different debates, see Higgins 2012, p.82-95. What is more, let us note that within the Dzogchen, *rang rig* is characterized by non-duality and the luminosity of knowledge (Higgins 2012, p.86 ; 95), and that according to Anne Burchardi, the 7th Karmapa connects *rang rig* with the *tathāgatagarbha* (Burchardi 2011, pp.317-344). She also gives different references on the interpretation of *rang rig* throughout history (Burchardi 2011, note 29 p.328).

canon and can be translated by "personally realized wisdom130." As David Higgins indicates, this term brings forward the mode of knowing the absolute – the mode of being of things is possible only through a direct perception[131]. The absolute must be lived amidst our own experience, there is no other alternative.

Meditative Exploration

Therefore, even if Buddha Nature is ineffable, it is not inaccessible. We only have to adopt a specific process to access it:

> They are "adamantine" (rDo rJe ; Vajra) since that which they point to is like a diamond, "hard" to penetrate via intellectual understanding without experiential realization due to their profundity, as well as being enduring "indestructible" truths applicable to the universe's abiding reality rather than culturally and linguistically dependent fabricated networks of conventional "truths". Thus right from the beginning this term points [...] to the quite different concept of a "text" here (which are phenomenological "reports" of lived experience meant to be re-lived via extra- textual contemplative means, as well as poetic philosophy). Germano 1992, p.51.

If we wish to access the meaning of Buddha Nature, intellectual understanding only is not sufficient. Indeed, this type of comprehension mainly solicits our mental consciousness. Yet, awakening

---

130 Or primordial knowledge.

131 "The compound can be rendered as 'primordial knowing as it is personally realized' where the *so sor rang rig pa 'i-°* (Skt. *pratyātmavid-°*) element of the compound is not intended adjectivally or nominatively but rather as a adverb-verb combination that qualifies the abstract noun *ye shes*. It expresses the rather old idea that the desired soteriological condition (in this case, *jñāna* but elsewhere the *paramārthasatya*, the *parinịspanna* etc.) must be 'personally experienced' to be fully understood. In other words, primordial knowing is a matter of direct acquaintance and not discoverable in any other fashion. Thus when the *vyākhyā* on *Ratnagotravibhāga* 1.7 characterizes "self-awareness" using the term *so so rang gis rig par bya ba* (*pratyātmavedanīya*), it is specifying a mode of awareness that must be personally realized to be known", Higgins 2012, p.88. On this term, see also Mathes 2008, note 1838 p.542.

calls for an integral "transformation" [132] engaging all aspects of our experience[133], and the latter is not limited to our mental consciousness. Experience also includes body and senses. Moreover, the relationship to mental consciousness will also be challenged. As David Germano explains in the above-mentioned excerpt, writings regarding Buddha Nature must be accompanied by an extra-textual dimension in order to give us a change to better apprehend it, and this dimension can be explored thanks to contemplative practices:

> The term "contemplatively take into your own experience" (Nyams Su Len Pa) indicates that ultimately the focus must not be on the mere "techniques" (though it is vital that you properly apply the various key points in accordance with contextualized guidance from someone who "has been there before"), but rather on the nature of the journey these techniques enable as you return back to the origins of the Universe itself. These systems of contemplation are precisely what make these texts so hermeneutically problematic in the West, since ultimately the text assumes an extra-textual dimension to the reader's interaction with it, i.e. s/he is actively engaged in its accompanying psycho- spiritual (and extremely specific) contemplative systems so as to fundamentally transform his/her physical and psychic energies. Germano 1992, p.114.

Similar to reasoning, the so-called "yogic" vision is considered valid according to the Buddhist epistemology[134] but is of a higher level. A certain destination is pointed to us as possible, for all, to the only condition that the practice is done:

---

132 It is more accurate to speak of a « change in state », see third part.

133 This presentation brings back to the Greek conception of philosophy as Pierre Hadot explains it. Philosophy is not only the elaboration of a discourse on the world, the true philosopher will seek to live this discourse through different spiritual exercises. See *Qu'est-ce que la philosophie antique,* ch.9 « Philosophie et discours philosophique. La philosophie et l'ambiguïté du discours philosophique » pp.265-275. On this topic, we can also consult the article « What is buddhist philosophy » in *Reason's traces* written by M. Kasptein (2001) or also V. Eltschinger, *Pierre Hadot et les « exercices spirituels » : quel modèle pour la philosophie bouddhique tardive ?* Asiatische Studien Études Asiatiques LXII 2, p.485-544 ; 2008.

134 See NY [80-81], Dunne 2006, Eltschinger 2009, Tillemans 2013.

> If you do not meditate on this dharma,
> you will not see the dharmatā.
> Just seeing and hearing about water,
> but not drinking, it doesn't alleviate thirst. *Moonbeams,* p.183.

This is about cultivating[135] new habits of perception that will permit seeing the absolute. « Bhāvanā » can also be translated by "to meditate" – to meditate in order to explore our own experience and change the mechanisms that plunge us into illusion. This learning of a new way-to-be applies to both body and consciousness – all dimensions of experience must be integrated since illusion is the result of a psycho-physical process.

Thus, this work will integrate in its reflection different techniques of meditation in relation to Rangjung Dorje's tradition. Accessing Buddha Nature remains impossible if we look at it from the "a third-person view" However, by including the subject's change in state in the analysis, we hope for an understanding of the studied topic that is less distant. This is why this study will seek to describe the different stages that one's consciousness must travel on the path in order to be conscious of its true nature.

Which path?

One last point must be touched on before starting this exploration: which path is to be followed?

During the presentation of the *Treatise on Pointing Out Buddha Nature,* it was established that the 3rd Karmapa associates Mahāmudrā with Buddha Nature, notably thanks to stanza 13 and the straightforwardness of the text in some parts. These two elements belong to the "Mahāmudrā of the essence," which can be considered as a direct or simultaneous[136] way. This type of path cannot be used

135 Sct. *bhāvanā*, tib. *sgom pa.*

136 Tib. *cig car ba*. R.A. Stein conduct a research study on the terms *cig car* and *rim gyis*, which translate the Chinese terms *t'ouen* (sudden) and *tsien* (gradual) in the work of Dunhuang. One add from his article is to show that *cig car* in Tibetan never has the meaning of "sudden" : « *Char* et *car* s'emploient couramment avec des noms de nombres pour désigner un groupe unitaire ou un ensemble clos de plusieurs éléments, par exemple *lnga-char* « all the five together », *gnyis-char* « tous les deux ensemble », etc. (Jäschke).

here since we must understand the different stages that one's consciousness must travel. As it happens, Rangjung Dorje also refers to this gradual process through the example of the beryl :

> [Let's take the example] of a beryl covered with stains
> Whose qualities, consequently, cannot appear.
> By purifying it with an alkaline solution and woven cloth,
> [Then], with an acidic solution and a wool fabric,
> [Finally] with pure water and [fine cotton] from Kāśī
> Through this purification, the beryl is a jewel source of accomplishment of all wishes.
> Consciousness is like beryl.
> To purify it from its three stains -
> [Obscurations] of afflictions, knowledge and absorptive meditation -,
> One must completely train on the paths of accumulation, unification
> On the seven impure bhūmis and the three pure bhūmis.
> Stanza 23-24 [111-121].

Consciousness is compared to a precious stone, the beryl[137]. Its purity and qualities are not recognized because of deposits that are classified in three categories: the obscurations linked to affliction, cognition, and meditative absorption. The veil of afflictions is the coarsest and includes all the mental poisons such as greed, anger, etc. The veil of the knowledgeable is the most subtle and includes the non-realization of all phenomenon's emptiness. The veil of meditative absorption is even more subtle. Jamgön Kong-

Aussi *gcig-car* (ou *char*) signifie-t-il « en une seule fois » et Jäschke traduit bien par « at the same time, simultaneously (opp. to one after the other, successively) » en citant le *mJangs-blun*. [...] Ni étymologiquement, ni pratiquement l'expression ne comporte l'acception « subite ». Tous les paradigmes concrets que j'ai pu trouver prouvent l'acception : « simultané ». [...] Indépendamment des notions philosophiques qui, elles, impliquent parfois la rapidité, il n'a pas l'acception « subit » . Stein 1971, p.14-17. See also Mathes 2008, note 196 p.436.

137 « A variety of emerald with the color of sea water », Dictionary le Littré. We also find the same example with gold, see. Gomez 1987.

trul Lodrö Thayé indicates that this includes torpor and agitation and also mentions the grasping of the four characteristics[138]. Their purification follows a progression described through the five paths and the ten bhūmis of awakening. After achieving of the paths of accumulation[139] and unification[140] where the veils of affliction are eradicated, the consciousness reaches the first bhūmis of awakening, which corresponds to the third path – the path of vision[141]. Then, consciousness purifies the veils of the knowledgeable on the seven first impure bhūmis, and the veils of meditative absorption on the three last pure bhūmis. This is the path of meditation[142]. Finally, consciousness reaches the path where there is nothing left to learn[143], where perceiving reality is effortless. Each path aims to develop specific awakening factors – there are thirty-seven of them in total[144], and each stage corresponds to a specific cognitive change. Yet, the *Treatise on Pointing Out Buddha Nature* does not give enough indications to elaborate a precise map of consciousness' evolution from the ordinary state to the awakened state according to this model[145].

The five paths and ten bhūmis are the elements of progression that are most evident in stanza 23 and 24. And yet, another indication of progress is also presented through the beryl's three layers of purification. Indeed, we can take note that in stance I.2 of the commentary of Asaṅga[146] in the *Supreme Continuum*, this purification is compared to the three "The Three Turnings of the Wheel." [147] In other words, we can suppose that the 3rd Karmapa reuses the hermeneutic proposed in the seventh chapter of the *Unveiling of*

138 Tib. *mtshan 'dzin bzhi.*

139 Tib. *tshogs lam.*

140 Tib. *sbyor lam.*

141 Tib. *mthong lam.*

142 Tib. *sgom lam.*

143 Tib. *mi slob lam.*

144 For details on these factors; Mipham, *Gateway to knowledge,* vol.III, 18.62-18.111. They are already cited in the pāli canon.

145 However, the study of *Abhisamayālaṃkāra (Ornament of Realization)* could perhaps be more relevant.

146 On the transmission in Tibet of the five treaties of Maitreya, see Brunnölzl, 2014 p.81-91.

147 Zhönu Pal also covers this example in his commentary of the *Supreme Continuum.* Originally, this comparison can be found in the *Dhāraṇīśvararājasūtra.* See Mathes, 2008, p. 228-234 and p. 369.

the Profound Meaning Sūtra [148] where the three Turnings are described. Unlike the five paths and ten bhūmis, it would be possible to apprehend the different states of consciousness by following this model and in accordance to the instructions specific to the Mahāmudrā of sutras[149], which is a gradual path[150]. In the work of the third Karmapa, elements about this topic are found not in the *Treatise on Pointing Out Buddha Nature* but in the *Aspiration Prayer of Mahāmudrā.* More explanations will be given in the introduction of the second part [of this book].

The situation of ordinary consciousness will first be studied. This foundation seems essential in order to understand what must be purified or deconstructed. Then, the key stages of progress towards awakening will be examined following the hermeneutic of the three "The Three Turnings of the Wheel" and the methods of the Mahāmudrā of sutras. By proceeding as so, it will be possible in a third time to attempt to explain the common points between all beings and the purification process.

The third Karmapa offers the key elements that the reader must understand in order to become aware of their situation, what is possible to realize and the means to attain Buddhahood. This text also evokes most of the major themes of Buddhism: the working of ordinary consciousness, emptiness, everything is consciousness... Every time, these will be approached mainly from the standpoint of experience. If debates have been conducted over the past centuries on certain notions, bibliographic references will be indicated as footnotes.

First part: Ordinary consciousness

During his first Sermon, the Buddha taught the Four Noble Truths. The first one describes the situation of ordinary beings:

> The Noble Truth of suffering (Dukkha) is this: Birth is suffering; aging is suffering; sickness is suffering; death is suffering; sorrow and lamentation, pain, grief and

148 Sct. *Saṃdhinirmocanasūtra*.

149 Or Mahāmudrā of the *pāramitās*, see Mathes 2006.

150 Tib. *rim gyis.*

> despair are suffering; association with the unpleasant is suffering; dissociation from the pleasant is suffering; not to get what one wants is suffering—in brief, the five aggregates of attachment are suffering. The First Sermon of the Buddha[151]

A first characteristic of this situation is suffering, *dukkha*[152]. The latter can be consecutive to birth, illness, aging, and death[153], to the state of being united with what we dislike, to be separate from what we love, or to not have what we desire[154]. But it is the last words of this first truth that seems most important, since they summarize what precedes them: "in brief, the five aggregates of attachment are suffering".[155] The five aggregates are a reference to the skandhas which designate the different components of the psycho-physical experience: forms, sensations, notions, mental formations, and [consciousnesses][156]. The third Karmapa takes up these ideas, notably in stanzas 10 and 11 of the *Treatise on Pointing Out Buddha Nature.*

What is the significance of this attachment and why does it generate suffering? Answering these two questions will allow for a better pinning down of ordinary consciousness's specificities.

Attachment to the five aggregates...

To understand what this attachment consists of, it is necessary to question ourselves on the nature of the "self." Indeed, the realiza-

151 Rahula, p.93.

152 *Dukkha* in pali, *duḥkha* in sanscrit, *sdug bsngal* in tibetan.

153 These four events are called « suffering of suffering » because of their obviously painful character. See Chapter 5 of *The Jewel Ornement of Liberation* written by Gampopa.

154 These three events are called « suffering of change » (ibid.).

155 This sentence could be related to the « omnipresent suffering » described by Gampopa (ibid.).

156 A description of the *skandhas* is located in the two main Abhidharma, that is to say the *Abhidharmakośa* from Vasubandhu and the *Abhidharmasamuccaya* from Asaṅga. The *Gateway to Knowledge* (tib. *mkhas jug)* of Mipham Rinpoche advantageoulsy brings together the essence of these two pieces of works. We can also find a description of the *skandha* of [consciosunesses] in the *Treatise on the Distinction between Consciousness and Wisdom* from Rangjung Dorje.

tion of "non-self" leads to liberation from suffering[157], and one of the functions of the teaching on the five aggregates is to refute the self[158]. What is, then, this self that must be denied to attain liberation?

The Fundamental Wisdom of the Middle Way (MMK[159]) from Nāgārjuna offers us a definition of the self in the fifteenth chapter:

> [...] Essence itself is not artificial And does not depend on another. (MMK, 15.2)[160].

The self does not depend on anything else than itself to exist. This type of self implies that a phenomenon must be independent from all causes and conditions since it exists by itself. It must also be indivisible. Indeed, if it was composed of parts, it would be dependent on other phenomena to exist. Finally, it must be permanent, it cannot be destroyed by time[161]. With this definition, the perception of a self points back to a substantial and necessarily dual vision of oneself and the world. The phenomena are separated from one another and each has a "substrate," the perceiving subject considering themselves separate from the world or external to what they perceive. This is then what is called dualistic grasping[162].

Whether in *The Fundamental Wisdom of the Middle Way* or the *Treatise on Pointing Out Buddha Nature*, the description of this experience of self is not well-developed. It seems however essential to question ourselves on the topic, if want to better understand later the experience of awakening, which, on the contrary, is founded

157 For a general presentation, see Walpola Rahula, chapter 6.

158 « If you desire to attain the discriminating knowledge that unmistakenly ascertains what should be known, you should study these ten topics which cause learnedness, as is taught in the great sutras and treatises. What are they? They are the ten topics of being learned in: 1) the aggregates; 2) the elements; 3) the sources; 4) dependent origination; 5) the correct and the incorrect; 6) the faculties; 7) time; 8) the truths; 9) the vehicles; 10) conditioned things and unconditioned things. By the power of gaining certainty in these ten topics, you will be freed from the delusions of unwholesome views that should be abandoned, such as banishing the ten types of self-oriented views and so forth, and you will increase the wisdom of things as they are and of all that exists ». Mipham 2007, Prologue.

159 Sct. *Mūlamadhyamaka kārikā*

160 J. Garfield 1995, p.221.

161 On the different types of self (sct. *svabhāva*), see Westerhoff 2009, p.20 et s.

162 Tib. *gnyis 'dzin*.

on the non-self. How is experienced the felt sense of an independent self, permanent and indivisible ? First, it will be necessary to examine the topic of experience, which is to say the "I," and then its perception of the world – and each case will be illustrated with the three characteristics of the self. The following developments will primarily be founded on communal experience.

Ordinary experience of "I" – the individual self

A dualistic approach implies first and foremost a perceiving subject that perceives itself as a self[163]. As soon as the self or me must be defined more precisely, it is not easy to see what "lies behind." When we say "I am," what does it corresponds to? Two elements can be brought forth in a first place – I am my body, and I am the one who thinks. The "I" is associated to a body and a consciousness.

Let's start with the body. Several relationships to the body are possible, and sometimes, consciousness of the body is not even present. But in general, the notion of a "self" implies that the body is perceived as belonging to me. It is not dependent on anything else that myself. We can define its contours and define it separately from other phenomena. The body is independent. Besides, even if we know that the body is transforming in every instant and destined to perish, ordinary consciousness maintains on the contrary an idea of permanence. The body is closely associated with our identity, and seeing its impermanence would come down to seeing its own death. Consciousness desires instead to maintain the ideas of the body' permanence and does not want the body to disappear or degrade. Also, the body is especially apprehended externally as a "whole." The body then appears to us as indivisible. In the case of pain, illnesses, or strong emotions, ordinary consciousness always maintains a dualistic approach. It stays at the surface of what it feels. What it feels is perceived as a block, against which it feels powerless.

Now, what does a substantial consciousness look like? Ordinary consciousness tends to separate body and consciousness. They are perceived as two distinct entities. Moreover, consciousness can

163 Tib. *'dzin pa*.

consider itself independent from the external world and would therefore be non-influenceable and have no role to play in what it sees. Even if we can intellectually doubt this absolute distinction, we live it as so – the links between consciousness, body, and the world are not always perceived. Ordinary consciousness also has the feeling that an "I" is present – it is almost holding back from each experience. Even if states of consciousness changed, there still would be the permanence of something that ensures what I am and my identity. Last and first names strengthen this perception. Despite the multiple changes of my body, opinions, and moods, I am always designated with the same name. This "I" not only ensures continuity; it is also constituted of specific traits – "I am this" or "I am that." There is therefore the feeling of a presence, of a permanent "I" with personal and immutable characteristics – "me." Even if I do not have the same aspect and the same thought than yesterday, there must be something that subsists in all these states so that I can apprehend myself as me and not anyone else. Finally, to illustrate indivisibility, we can take the example of the relationship to thoughts. Consciousness is under the impression that its thoughts are evident. The latter do not have thickness or depth: "I think" is indivisible. The felt experience does not have any background, there is nothing else to see than what is seen in the first place.

Ordinary experience of the world – the self of phenomena.

Dualistic grasping is also relevant to the perception of the world[164]. This "I" positions itself in front of a world that it considers external to itself. Since consciousness can see only what it thinks and feels, the latter cannot be outside of itself. Therefore, if consciousness considers itself substantial, the rest of the world will appear under this form as well: other people are also individuals with *one* body and *one* consciousness, and objects have an existence and properties that are theirs only.

"I," the other "I's," and objects exist within a space that itself has a "self." The grasping of space's self means that it is independent of perception. At the ordinary level, space is only an empty container able to welcome subjects and things. We could event say

164 Tib. *gzung ba*.

that space is delimited by perceived phenomena, since ordinary consciousness rarely notices empty space. Space is "nothing," only its content grabs the attention. Space is therefore narrowed down to the contours of ordinary perception. The notion of "self" also has an incidence on the conception of time. Life is ruled by a time that is divided in years, days, hours.... Time is therefore reduced to units that can be counted. Additionally, consciousness organizes its existence according to past, present, and future. Grasping time like a self ends up being like trusting this external and measurable time, and to follow the sequence from past to present to future. This configuration of time seems permanent, indivisible, and independent. Time is like "given." Finally, one last aspect in the grasping of a self at an external level can be evoked through relations and laws. In order to be able to live in this space, it is essential for consciousness to understand how it functions, how phenomena interact inside of it. If consciousness has no knowledge of this functioning, its existence will be left to chance, to uncertainty. Laws like causality are therefore sought for in order to better apprehend the world, have landmarks, and thus better manage one's life. Once these relations are identified, consciousness tends to continually rely on them.

The causes of dualistic grasping

Many factors contribute to the existence of dualistic grasping. First of all, Jamgön Kongtrul Lodrö Thayé explains that it is generated by tendencies[165] without beginning:

> Still, due to the power of beginningless latent tendencies unfolding,
>
> [both apprehender and apprehended] appear. NTC, Stance 11, in *Luminous Heart p.213.*

It is therefore out of habit that consciousness perceives phenomena in this way. Consciousness finds it normal, since it has been in this

165 The tendencies can be manifest or latent.

configuration for all this time without beginning, which is to say forever[166]. This is also referred as innate ignorance[167]. From the instant that one of our senses is activated, there is a tendency to "objectify." To feel, see, hear, feel, or taste gives us the impression that we are interacting with a material world that is foreign to us, matter resists us. Senses are gripping before any mental activity, and the feeling of separation starts at the senses' door.

In addition to this exists the sharing of knowledge with others, language, and even the efficacy of laws. All of these factors give a feeling of objectivity and presence to a world that exists independently from consciousness. In this case, we speak of imagined ignorance[168]. Let's take the example of language. It is indispensable to communicate and transmit, and the repeated use of words lead us to think that words are things[169].

Furthermore, words also give meaning. As soon as a word is pronounced, a meaning becomes evident. Consequently, a certain reading grid of the world is transmitted to us, most often unconsciously, and it conditions our ways of living. Language takes us back to a world that is ready to use according to certain rules that are based on the notion of a self[170].

---

166 The notion of "without beginning" means here that it is not possible to find an origin to dualistic grasping – it is present from birth and was already present in several past lives. This grasping reflects *karma*. Another meaning is given in stanza 4 of the *Treatise on Pointing Out Buddha Nature.*

167 Tib.*lhan cig skyes pa'i ma rig pa*.

168 Tib. *kun brtags ma rig pa*.

169 Sakya Paṇḍita explains that language is in reality the result of two forms of abstraction – it unites that which is different (generalizing function) and distinguishes that which maintains itself together (differentiating function) see Hugon, 2008, *Rigs gter* IV [222.121.1] et [222.122.1].

170 « Quelle que soit la variété des langues ou des patois, ce qui compte c'est que l'enfant reçoit, à son insu, des clés, un code, une grille de lecture qui permettra peu à peu de structurer et d'organiser ses expériences. Par exemple : *où, quand, qui, quoi, combien*, etc. Aristote a ainsi recensé dix « figures de prédication » [...] plus connues sous le nom de catégories. A-t-on, aussi, suffisamment remarqué l'initiation à une mentalité archétypale qu'opèrent les livres d'images : voici le cheval, le lion, la maison etc. Même chose pour les adultes se promenant dans un zoo, chaque fois qu'il y a un seul exemplaire d'une espèce animale. Tout cela installe peu à peu l'enfant à son insu, dans le *saṃvṛtisatya* [vérité superficielle]. [...] C'est pourquoi nous pouvons vivre dans le monde des ustensiles, le *vyavahāra,* sans même le savoir, et prendre implicitement les mots pour des choses, ignorer que le langage est un code et que nous fonctionnons d'après lui ». Bugault 1994, p.328-329. These descriptions are primarily relevant to communal experience and the superficial truth.

Conclusion

Dualistic grasping of ordinary consciousness therefore appears in different forms. Duality exists at an individual level, which itself comes in different forms of duality. Consciousness and body are perceived as two different entities, without any relationship between the two. Duality also manifests within consciousness itself. Indeed, my own experience can be lived as separate. In this case, duality is not only between a subject and an external object anymore, it is also located within the subject itself. An "I" looks at a "thought" or an emotion as if they were different from itself. There is an internal duplication, a dissociation. Furthermore, when an "I" considers itself like a self, it is automatically separate from the rest of the manifestation. It is not linked, since it considers itself as independent from its surroundings. Others, objects, space, or even time are external to consciousness, having their own existence. There is therefore duality between the individual self and the rest of the phenomena.

The five aggregates do not correspond to the definition of the self, they are even at the opposite. Instead of presenting an independent experience, indivisible and permanent, the *skandhas* show on the contrary that the whole of experience can be decomposed in different elements, and it changes in each instant. Thus, attaching to or grasping onto the five aggregates means having an erroneous perception of that which truly is. Ordinary consciousness is then illusioned, its "view" is not accurate. The grasping of a self condemns consciousness to stay at the surface of experience, therefore the perception is gross or incomplete[171]. Consciousness is plunged in ignorance, *ma rig pa* in Tibetan. « Ma » marks negation, and « rig pa » designates the true nature of consciousness.

... is source of suffering

Illusion does not limit itself to an inaccurate knowledge of reality, since attachment to the five aggregates is a source of different dissatisfactions encountered during existence. Grasping a "self" is only the fruit of ignorant imagination – and yet, it causes *saṃsāra* :

171 Tib. *rnam pa.*

Because of ignorant imagination
It is the *saṃsāra*. NT, Stanza 8 [29-30].

When the 3rd Karmapa describes ordinary consciousness, he attributes two aspects to the mental – immediate aspect and afflicted aspect[172]. The immediate aspect ensures the continuity of different instants of consciousness, it ensures their unity. As for the other aspect of the mental, it is a source of affliction:

The [other] part of this, with regard to mind as such,
Entails self-centeredness, holding on to pride[173],
Attachment to "me," and ignorance.
Since it produces all [views about] the perishing collection,
It is called "the afflicted mind"[174]. NY [82–86], in *Luminous Heart p. 284.*

Since the immediate aspect is accompanied with the afflicted aspect, self-grasping is present in each instant. We thus find here again the idea that attachment causes suffering.

At stanza 10, we understand that ignorant imagination is constituted by mental formations[175]:

By mental formations, comparable to the wind
Karma and afflictions are produced
By [mental formations], *skandhas, dhātus* and āyatanas,
All phenomena that appear in a dual form are manifested.

---

172 NY, Stanza 10. The functioning of ordinary consciousness is described through eight aspects : the five sensory consciousnesses, mental consciousness, the mental or « seventh consciousness » that itself has two facets, and the *ālayavijñāna*. On this topic, see the *rnam shes ye shes 'byed pa'i bstan bcos* (*Treatise on the Distinction between Consciousness and Wisdom)* and Brunnhölzl 2009.

173 The Abhidharma distinguishes seven types of prides. The central idea is to consider oneself superior to others. See *Gateway to Knowledge*, 1.63 (Volume 1).

174 *Ngar sems nga rgyal 'dzin pa dang/ Nga la chags shing ma rig bcas/ 'jig tshogs thams cad bskyed pa'i phyir/*
Nyon mongs can gyi yid ces bya/

175 sct. *saṃskāra*, tib. '*du byed*. Several translations have been proposed for *saṃskāra*, and the term which was retained is « mental formation ». See. Kapani L., *La notion de saṃskāra dans l'Inde brahmanique et bouddhique,* Collège de France, 1992.

NT, Stanza 10 [34-37].

Mental formations are the origin of *karma,* afflictions, and all phenomena. In other words, they are the origin of *saṃsāra.*

Mental formations

Mental formations or *saṃskāras* designate the fourth *skandha.* « Saṃ » means « aggregate» and « kāra » means « shape, create ». The *saṃskāras* are represented in the Wheel of Life by a potter fabricating his pot[176]. Mental formations can be defined as so:

> Objectively, this appears as the realm of possibilities, subjectively as the realm of tendencies, a potential for action and mobilization. [...] The *saṃskāra-skandha* represents a realm of forces inherited from past actions, near or remote, and which spring into action again when new circumstances arise. The individual assumes - or re-assumes - this potential, sometimes in a deliberate and voluntary manner, sometimes without their knowing under the form of pulsions[177], Kapani 1992, p.180[178].

The *saṃskāras* are the aggregates of the tendencies or influences of an individual that are constituted over time. What we perceive out of reality is the result of our education, language, society in which we live, relationships. We also build or constitute our reality on the basis of what we feel, as the omnipresent factor of sensation (second *skandha*) indicates. Thus, *saṃskāras* are the fruit of our past experience and form the image of the "self" and the "world," like a potter making his pot. We are *saṃskāras.*

---

176 See Representation of the second *nidāna* or link on the Wheel of Life.

177 « Objectivement, cela se présente comme le champ du possible, subjectivement comme le champ des tendances, un potentiel d'action et de mobilisation. [...] Le *saṃskāra-skandha* représente un champ de forces héritées des actes passés, proches ou lointains, et qui entrent en action de nouveau à l'occasion de nouvelles circonstances. L'individu assume, ou réassume, ce potentiel, tantôt d'une manière délibérée et volontaire, tantôt à son insu sous forme de pulsions ».

178 The signification of the term *saṃskāra* is complex and the texts of the 3rd Karmapa do not give us enough elements to treat this subject exhaustively. For further developments, see Kapani (1992).

The *Treatise on the Distinction between Consciousness* and *Wisdom* specifies that the five consciousnesses as well as the first instant of the sixth consciousness are without concepts[179], because their respective objects are perceived without being identified. For example, visual consciousness sees the color blue, but does not think "it's blue"[180]. These six consciousnesses simply registers the object – the sound, the form, etc. – without naming it. But the next instant, mental consciousness enters a phase of recognition of the different characteristics of the object, and these are determined by mental formations :

> Consciousness is what perceives objects,
> While the formations of mental factors [perceive their] features,
> Which is based on the mental consciousness[181]. NY [72-74] in *Luminous Heart*, p.281.

Once the presence of the object is registered, the information received is shaped by the different mental events listed within this fourth *skandha*[182].

It is now necessary to clarify the link between *saṃskāras* and afflictions, *saṃskāras* and *karma*, and *saṃskāras* and phenomena, in order to understand how the grasping of a self is intrinsically linked to the *saṃsāra.*

Saṃskāras and afflictions

The afflictions have already been evoked in the description of the afflicted mental. It is not emotions such as anger, joy, or jealousy which are targeted, but the relationship existing between ordinary

179 Tib. *rtog med.*

180 Brunnhölzl, 2009, p.281.

181 *Don mthong rnam par shes yin kyang/ Khyad par sems byung 'du byed ni/ Yid kyi rnam shes la brten te/*
The verses [72-73] are also mentioned in *Madhyāntavibhāga* I.8cd. « *mthong* » rather signifies perceiving. Yet, we translated it by « receiving» to emphasize the difference with conceptual consciousness.

182 See *Gateway to Knowledge* Vol.1, 1.31-1.134, to consult the full list of the *saṃskāras*.

consciousness and these states. In order to establish a link between the self-grasping and afflictions, let's focus on the way that ordinary consciousness acts to find satisfaction.

Happiness according to ordinary consciousness

Dualistic grasping implies a certain conception of the body, consciousness, and the world. Everything is ruled by the notion of a substantial self. The way that consciousness projects its existence will therefore be based on this same principle. More precisely, the *saṃskāras* are reference points onto which consciousness leans onto to develop projects, to realize its dreams.

Its attitude entails adopting what seems beneficial and rejecting what seems harmful to its blossoming[183]. This principle is the equivalent of the three poisons[184], symbolized by the rooster, the hog[185], and the snake in the middle of the Wheel of Life. They are the hub, the heart of each of our actions. Adoption and rejection are done depending on the image that the consciousness has of itself and the world inside of which it lives. According to the different *saṃskāras* accumulated over time, consciousness identifies what is good and bad for itself. The *saṃskāras* shape an ideal of happiness, and the existential strategy rests on defending that image, which includes simultaneously ourselves, our relationships, our projects, our beliefs, our material possessions, etc. Everything that contributes to its embellishment and expansion is adopted (friends, accumulation of material goods or power for example), otherwise consciousness is in rejection or indifference. I ignore what does not bring me anything, I desire what I want, and I reject what threatens me. This is the ego's fundamental strategy, which is to say a consciousness that grasps a self. In other words, adoption, rejection, and indifference define the desire to exist of an ordinary consciousness.[186].

183 NT, stance 11.

184 Tib. *dug gsum* : desire – passion (tib. *dod chags*), hate –aversion (tib. *zhe sdang*) and indifference – ignorance (tib. *gti mug*).

185 This is a hog, not pork. The latter is a domesticated animal, while the former is a wild animal.

186 Thus, the origin of suffering is explained by egoic desire, not by any type of desire (see second noble truth, Walpola Rahula p.29 and s.).

The eight mundane *dharmas* also describe this mechanism – the hope for profit and fear of loss, the hope for pleasure and the fear of displeasure, the hope for fame and the fear of disgrace, the hope for praise and the fear of blame – all ordinary actions are based on hope[187] and fear[188] .

The three poisons reflect the attitude of consciousness that places itself at the center of a world which it strives to preserve. What is considered to be "self" – consciousness, body, but also all the people and goods that contribute to nourish our existence – must be conserved, even developed. This type of attitude characterizes a search for happiness based on a "conquest" of the external world. Ordinary consciousness seeks to blossom through possession, it needs to set up certain situations that will provide well-being.

However, according to Buddhism, this way of existing cannot lead to lasting satisfaction. It is not possible to be exhaustive on the different reasons that can lead to dissatisfaction, only some mechanisms will be brought forward in the following sections, in order to show the link between the self-grasping and dissatisfaction.

Aging, illness, and death

Grasping onto the body means believing in its permanence, thus the body partly constitutes our "me." Thus, aging, illness, and death can be painful and generate different afflictions. Even if we age with each passing instant, this does not imply that that we are in adequation with the process. Not only aren't we necessarily aware that our body constantly changes but knowing that we are aging also doesn't imply accepting such aging. There can be some difficulty in accepting the passing of time, accepting the impermanence of the body – either for esthetical reasons or because time passing enables us to do fewer and fewer things over the years. The body can also be sick, moreover implicating physical pain and incapacitation. With a gross understanding of the body, it can be difficult to cope. Amidst pain, grasping can contribute to maintaining and nourishing such pain. Eventually, death can also be experienced as suffering by referring us back to the loss of what we think to be "me."

187 Sct. *āśā*, tib. *re ba.*

188 Sct. *saṃbadhā*, tib. *dogs pa.*

Impermanence

Ordinary consciousness is not sure to obtain what it wishes, which is a source of affliction. Subsequently, even if it obtains what it wants, the latter cannot last eternally, since everything that is born dies. Sooner or later, what we possess is doomed to disappear. If consciousness grasps strongly to its reference points, it will have more difficulties facing the ineluctable law of impermanence. The more consciousness fixes its world, the greater its dissatisfaction when the discrepancy between desire and reality manifests. Since time never stops and all phenomena are in constant transformation, a discrepancy between what we think is and what actually is necessarily arises. This discrepancy can lead to dissatisfaction because our aspirations are not fulfilled, creating also a loss of meaning. As soon as the course of events does not comply anymore with our keys for understanding, our world views, consciousness is disoriented. Forgetting time leads to lacking flexibility while facing existence and a lack of stability while facing change. What is more, primarily depending on the external world to be happy means that is not possible to be the master of a situation, since nothing is certain, nothing is predictable. When well-being depends on external causes, even the slightest change can disrupt it. Afflictions are then born from the non-obtention of what is desired or the loss of what is acquired.

Endless quest

Yet, also, without speaking of phenomena's temporality, ordinary consciousness accomplishes sometimes better itself through the necessary process of realizing this or that project. Thus, once it obtains what it desires, a type of boredom, anguish, or emptiness can settle in, because the object which it was turning towards is obtained. It is the waiting of the desired object rather than the obtention of the object which is aimed at. Consciousness amidst resting is lost, it then searches for a new direction, a new goal, it is searching for this tension towards the sought-after object, because consciousness is afraid of void. Consequently, the search is endless. As soon as one desire is fulfilled, another must follow. This quest never ends. From a more internal perspective, this signifies that consciousness is never at rest, in the present, it is always tensed between past and future.

Conditioning

Besides, the self-grasping leads to conditioning, since ordinary seeing is determined by *saṃskāras*. This implies a certain view of the self and the world, and finding an alternative to our view is difficult. Consciousness is shaped, conditioned by the education received, the language in which it expresses itself, the habits of its society, the people met. If consciousness stays at the surface of what it sees, the odds of living a life that is not its own are great. Its life choices will be limited to what it learns without seeking to know whether such choices really fit. Failing to realize oneself implies that a part of ourselves has not received sufficient attention, in which case true blossoming cannot happen, and this can also breed frustration or some sort of slight dissatisfaction in our life.

Conditioning also implies reduced possibilities of existence, and our life almost becomes predictable. Indeed, when consciousness is configured by *saṃskāras*, the world in which it resides is closed and repetitive. *Saṃskāras* represent a type of configuration in a given situation. In the past, consciousness reacted in a certain way in a specific context - and consciousness has a tendency to register or freeze this or that reaction. It takes a particular shape, which it will manifest again when a similar situation presents itself. The other possibilities for response are not explored, the present becomes past, the present becomes a repetition of the past. And what we think is the future will only be a ramification of the past. Ordinary consciousness maintains itself on this line, past present future, which is in reality the repetition of the same thing. The events are perhaps different, but the undercurrent themes are identical. Everything that presents itself is interpreted in relation to the story that consciousness created. Every event that arises takes its place in a story, and consciousness arranges the whole to make it coherent. Thus, once the main interpretations are established, ordinary consciousness can become predictable. It does not have the time or the means to discover other ways of seeing.

This way of acting imprisons us. By blindly following the structures that seem well-established, the cogs of the process are completely ignored. There is no room for maneuver, it is enough to press on a button to get a reaction. Experience resembles a ping pong game – the ball is barely received that it is already sent back. Then these habits influence and mutually strengthen each other, again and again plunging ordinary consciousness into *saṃsāra*.

Saṃskāras, karma and phenomena

Saṃskāras and *karma*

Saṃskāras breed afflictions but also karma. *Saṃskāras* are the different mental formations that constitute our perception, and karma designates first and foremost action. *Saṃskāras* are our tendencies, our psychic dispositions, and karma is their materialization, the acting out of the three poisons. Karma designates the action as a whole, the action of creating something, and saṃskāras give the keys for understanding these actions.

Therefore, *saṃskāras* and *karma* are intimately linked: *saṃskāras* condition *karma*, and *karma* also conditions *saṃskāras*. Let's note that one of Buddhism's specificities is to insist on the importance of intention[189] when an action is taken:

> Monks, I say that intention is acting; by intention, one performs an action of body, speech, or mind, Aṅguttaranikāya, III, 415 in Dennis Hirota, 2005.

Therefore, it is not the action itself that conditions the future, but the intention that determines the quality of the action[190].

At the very moment of our action, a certain pattern concretizes, a certain way of seeing looks for a way to realize its purpose. If no reassessment is done, then the *saṃskāras* which are at the origin of the action strengthen, because they will have the possibility to

189 Sct. *cetanā*, tib. *sems pa*.

190 "It is the intention functioning as the motive force giving rise to deeds that determines their quality and thus their karmic effect. Hence, harm inflicted inadvertently does not necessarily bespeak an evil act entailing unwholesome retribution, and even meritorious acts may in fact be injurious", Hirota D. 2005.

once again assert themselves. Besides, when an affliction arises, ordinary consciousness will tend to address it in a dualistic way. The affliction is perceived as external, as something that does not really belong to us. This affliction will be either rejected or ignored, or might take space within consciousness itself, which will not know what to do with it. When consciousness' perception is completely veiled, its own interiority is inaccessible. Situations slip away from it, and consciousness does not react appropriately. Consciousness is under pressure, tensed, and if an event happens, the reaction is automatic. Thus, the principles that consciousness follows breed afflictions, and its meeting with afflictions generates even more afflictions.

We are therefore in the presence of a process that is conditioned-conditioning. *Saṃskāras* are the result of past actions, and they condition future actions. What we are today is the result of past acts, and what we will be is the result of what we do today.

Saṃskāras et phénomènes

Karma was previously considered in terms of actions only. Yet, the meaning of karma is not only that of naming action, it also points to the set of the causes and consequences that condition the existence of a being, both in this life and future ones. The body is the fruit of karma, life situations are the fruit of karma – all phenomena are the fruit of karma.[191]. *Karma* and *saṃsāra* come together.

These different claims cannot be demonstrated. One can observe that these phenomena arise in a causal way – "we reap what we sow" – but ordinary vision cannot go too deeply into the mechanisms of causality. Only a buddha can perceive it, as Jamgön Mipham describes:

191 « This process of rebirth is guided and even generated by the force of a person's actions (karman), which possess the power of inevitably working their consequences. Thus, deeds in the present will unfailingly bear their fruit in this or a future life, and present conditions, pleasurable or disagreeable, including one's form of existence, length of life, social station, and personal appearance, are the effects of deeds performed in the past. The span of one's existence through cycles of birth and death (saṃsāra) stretches back endlessly into the past and will continue without limit into the future, unless liberation is attained ». Hirota 2005, p.5097.

> Some people try to analyze the functioning of the karmic law and try to explain logically why certain actions give certain effects. When they fail to do so, there is the danger that they might go completely astray and conclude that the karmic principle in itself is absurd. Consequently, in view of the fact that the karmic principle cannot be proved on the basis of limited human experience, the Buddha said that karma was inconceivable and discouraged attempts to investigate it. For it is indeed difficult to penetrate such a profound topic.[192]

Adoption and rejection do not lead to satisfaction

As long as self-grasping still exist, suffering will be omnipresent. In other words, it is not the different events of life that are painful in themselves, but dukkha is the fruit of a wrong relationship to the self, of an excessive attachment to something that does not intrinsically exist. It is this relationship that leads an individual into an endless cycle of situations experienced as unfavorable and painful.

Stanza 11 from the *Treatise on Pointing Out Buddha Nature* summarizes the link between the self-grasping and dissatisfaction. Since everything is the reflection of consciousness – everything is *saṃskāra* - the attitude of adopting and rejecting perceived objects cannot provide durable satisfaction :

> By rejecting our own appearances, where will they cease?
>
> By adopting our own appearances, what appears? NT, Stanza 11, [39-40] [193]

Indeed, everything that is perceived is considered as different from the perceiving subject, whereas deeper analysis reveals on the contrary that everything is consciousness only, everything is projec-

---

192 *Madhyamakāvatāra*, translation from English - Introduction to the middle way: Candrakīrti's *Madhyamakāvatāra*, with commentary by Ju Mipham, Stanza 42, p.227.

193 See Brunnhölzl 2009, note 522

tion[194]. In this case, the illusion entails objectifying or considering as "other" that which is the fruit of my own cognitive activity. Similarly, in dreams, our own consciousness is perceived as foreign. Yet, the perceiving subject and the perceived object are in reality two aspects of the same consciousness:

> Like the ignorant who not recognising the rope take it for a snake, people imagine an external world, not knowing that it is of Mind itself.
> LKV, Sagāthakam, 498 in Suzuki 2009, p.262.

By rejecting, we say "not this," "I do not want it." But when will appearances cease? We are rejecting a form of reality and values that are only the reflection of karmic impressions. Even if we avoid the given object, the reasons that lead us to reject it will not cease. We think that it is the object that is the source of our dissatisfaction and dismiss it, but it is rather what we project on it that is responsible for the situation. As long as the origin of rejection is not perceived, what displeases us will continue to manifest.

By adopting an object that is in fact our own projection, what do we gain? We adopt this or that thing thinking that satisfaction will be reached. We have previously seen what follows this particular alternative. More fundamentally, this strategy of adopting cannot bear fruits, because what we adopt in reality is the representation of the object that we have chosen, which necessarily displays discrepancies with what really is. The origin of this anticipation anchors itself in a "me" that is not in accordance with what is real. There is therefore a rejection of the real from the beginning, we want the world to be as we desire it to be.

By continuing to act on the basis of the three poisons or adoption and rejection, consciousness faces continuous dissatisfaction, because deep and continuous satisfaction does not arise. The notions of good or bad are only located in consciousness. Nothing ceases because our tendencies for aversion remain, strengthen, and

194 Tib. *rang snang*. The example of the dream is often used as an illustration (for example see NY [49-52]). For a more extensive explanation, it is appropriate to consult the Indian texts of the Yogācāra. B. Chaterjee in his work *The Yogācāra Idealism* identifies the different arguments destined to refute the idea of realism (chapters 3 et 4); see also Brunnhölzl 2009, *Introduction* p.1-124.

nothing appears because the source of sustainable contentment cannot be found in perishable objects.

Dualistic grasping conditions our vision of the world and all aspects of our existence, it is source of *dukkha*.

Second part : Awakened consciousness

THE END OF *SAṂSĀRA* IS POSSIBLE

To ordinary consciousness, dualistic grasping seems normal – yet, this way of seeing is only illusion[195], deception[196]. The perception of a substantial self is creation of consciousness only, constituted of different veils, distinguished into the veil of affliction and the veil of the knowledgeable[197]. The *Supreme Continuum* compares it to clouds:

> By nature not existent, pervasive,
> and adventitious, the veils of the poisons
> and of the hindrances to knowledge
> are described as being similar to a cloud[198]. *Buddha nature,* p.44.

This comparison to clouds shows that despite appearances, what is perceived is not as substantial or solid as it seems, as this citation from Saraha confirms:

> When wind hits water and whips it up,
> Even soft water can turn to stone.
> When whipped up by thoughts,
> Formless confusion can become solid and hard. *Moonbeams,* p.239

195 Tib. *'khrul pa.*

196 Tib. *rdzun ma* ; NT, Stanza 11 [41].

197 There are also veils related to meditative absorption (see NTC, Stanza 36), in particular agitation and torpor (*Moonbeams*, p.195 and following). These will not be treated in this study since meditation is only addressed to better understand the steps of the self-deconstruction.

198 *Rang bzhin gyis ni ma grub dang/ Khyab dang glo bur ba nyid kyis/ Nyon mongs shes bya'i sgrib pa der/ Sprin dang 'dra bar brjod pa yin/*

Ordinary consciousness tends to solidify what it perceives to the point of taking what it sees as absolute. However, nothing is fixed, *saṃsāra* is only a reunion of different tendencies[199]. That is why ordinary consciousness is not the only possible mode of perception, *saṃsāra* have an end[200]. As soon as the veils are purified, another mode of being reveals itself, *nirvāṇa*:

> This purity itself is now present.
> Despite its presence, we do not perceive it
> Because of ignorant imagination
> It is the saṃsāra.
> If this in itself is purified, *nirvāṇa* manifests itself.
> It is conventionally designated as the end. NT, Stanza 8-9 [28-32].

Nirvāṇa corresponds to the actualization of Buddha Nature – in other words, *nirvāṇa* is the realization of Buddhahood. *Saṃsāra* is conventionally designated as the end. Indeed, if *saṃsāra* does not have a truly existing self, it neither has an end. Its end is only relative, which is to say conventional. The end of *saṃsāra* is only the end of a point of view on superficial truth – in reality, all phenomena are without beginning nor end from an absolute standpoint.

How to go from solidity to flexibility? Which process unveils consciousness?

THE THREE TURNINGS

The three turnings of the wheel are exposed in the *Unveiling of the Profound Meaning Sūtra,* where the Buddha answers the questions of Paramārthasamudgata, who is perplexed towards apparent contradictions in the teachings. Indeed, the Buddha declares that the skandhas exist intrinsically, but he also declares that phenomena are emptiness. After a couple of exchanges, Paramārthasamudgata understands the intention of the Buddha. He then proposes a

199 NTC, Stanza 4.
200 NT, Stanzas 1 and 9.

classification of his teachings that follows the progression of consciousness on the path. Each turning corresponds to a determined realization, which is exceeded by the following turning[201].

The meaning of the first turning is clear, it corresponds to the Four Noble Truths. The first turning of the wheel is thus associated with the arhats' realization of self-emptiness[202]. From a Mahāyāna standpoint, it is the veils of affliction that are mainly purified at this stage[203]. On the other hand, the second and third turnings seem fairly similar, since they present a priori the same thesis – all phenomena are emptiness. Yet, there must be a difference, as the third turning has been turned to go beyond the limits of understanding of the second one. John Powers explains that the meaning of the third turning largely depends on the context. It is not possible to determine such meaning solely from the text of the *Unveiling of the Profound Meaning Sūtra*, and it is relative to the meaning that is given to the first two turnings[204].

The veils of the knowledgeable (or cognitive veils) are dissolved by the realization of emptiness. Two types of interpretation are envisioned in the *Treatise on Pointing Out Buddha Nature* – emptiness

201 Lamotte, 1935, p.85 ; 206-207 ; Powers 1994, p.138-141. For a summarized presentation of this sūtra, see Lopez 1988, p. 56-59. For a detailed presentation, see Powers, 2004 (1993).

202 The term « *arhat* » is particularly important in the Theravāda tradition since it designates the highest spiritual state: it designates the one who reached enlightenment, *nirvāṇa*. « *Arhat* » in Sanskrit literally signifies "the one who deserves to be praised." As for the Tibetan « *dgra bcom,* » it signifies « the one who destroyed the enemy». The enemy represents affliction. Thanks to their accomplishment of the thirty-seven factors of awakening, the *arhat* attains freedom of consciousness and heart, they overcame desire, passion, and they developed a real knowledge that allowed them to go beyond *saṃsāra* (See Swearer Donald K., "Arhat", in *Encyclopedia of Religion,* 2nd Edition Thomson Gale, p. 476-478, 1987).

203 In the *Supreme Continuum*, the nine examples presented in the *vajra* point of the *dhātu* brings us back to the progression of well-defined states of consciousness, with their associated veils (RGV I. 130-143/114-124). The first four examples pertain to ordinary consciousness – the decaying lotus, the honey and bees, the seed in its husk, the gold in filth. The decaying of the lotus points to desire, the bees to anger, the husk to ignorance, and the tattered rag to the desire towards those who are liberated from desire. The fifth example, the one of the treasure buried under the house of a destitute man, pertains to the *arhats*. The soil that covers the treasure symbolizes ignorance and karmic tendencies. Therefore, from the standpoint of the nine examples, the *arhats* have purified the afflictions but the cognitive veils are still present.

204 Powers, 2004 (1993), p.133. He also exposes in chapter 5 other interpretations than those studied here.

as intellectual understanding[205], and emptiness stemming from the Mahāmudrā meditation[206]. These two distinctions can already be found in India, notably in the *Tattvadaśaka* written by Maitrīpa. In the commentary of this text, Sahajavajra identifies intellectual understanding of emptiness as the analytical path proposed by Kamalaśīla, and he explains that the absolute can be realized by developing a non-analytical mind[207]. Zhönu Pal also uses this distinction[208]:

> Among the *Bodhisattvas*, [some] find the emptiness of non-affirming negation through inferential valid cognition, but even this valid cognition is taken to be ignorance inasmuch as it is conceptual by nature. Therefore, here, the manner of the last *dharmacakra* is supreme, because you are mainly engaged in the nonconceptual. DRSM, 438.23-6. Mathes 2008, p.377.

Consequently, we will link to the second turning the intellectual understanding of emptiness[209], and to the third the direct perception of emptiness.

205 NT, stanza 12.

206 NT, stanza 13. In reality, the whole set of texts is involved. But we mention stanza 13 in particular because it follows the presentation of emptiness as intellectual understanding, and it is also the only stanza where the Mahāmudrā practice is clearly indicated through the terms of "natural consciousness."

207 « [...] In this [*Bhāvanākrama*] it is not pure, having been produced on the basis of analysis, whereas here [in the *Tattvadaśaka*] it must be directly meditated upon with a non-analytical mind ». Mathes 2008, p.38.

208 We cite Zhönu Pal because his commentary of the *Supreme Continuum* follows the same line of interpretation as that of Rangjoung Dorjé. They both inscribe themselves amidst the meditative tradition and the practice Mahāmudrā practice (Mathes, 2008, Preface, p.x). Nonetheless, we must note that Zhönu Pal does not take on the same hermeneutic strategy as that of the 3rd Karmapa. He rather bases his interpretation of Buddha Nature on the *Laṅkāvatārasūtra*.

209 Also named as "non-affirmative negation." This identification between non-affirmative negation and intellectual understanding of emptiness is not right in all cases. Indeed, Ngog Loden Sherab interprets Buddha Nature as a non-affirmative negation while agreeing to say that the absolute is not accessible via inferences only. Mathes 2008, p.2 ; 25-32.

Mahāmudrā of sūtras

The passage from one turning to the other will be studied in the light of the instructions of the Mahāmudrā sūtras. Contrary to the Mahāmudrā of essence that is a direct approach, the way of the sūtras will gradually lead us towards awakened consciousness by indicating what ordinary consciousness needs to go through to access the absolute.

In the work of the 3rd Karmapa, it is the *Aspiration Prayer of Mahāmudrā* which offers the largest number of information in that regard. Indeed, after wishing in stanza 15 to maintain himself within the nature of consciousness, in natural consciousness, the author goes on evoking the meditations of mental calm and penetrating vision. What is more, at the beginning of this text, he mentions the accumulation of merits, the precious human body, trust, or spiritual friend. All these themes are expanded upon in the *The Jewel Ornement of Liberation* from Gampopa, a work of reference in the Kagyü lignage regarding the gradual path[210]. This work enumerates the different causes and conditions necessary to reach awakening, as well as the different practices to take on. Awakening is possible because all beings have the cause of awakening, which is to say Buddha Nature (Chapter 1). However, the conditions must be present in order to reveal it. These conditions are the precious human existence and the presence of a spiritual friend (chapters 2 and 3). Then, the chapters describe preliminary reflections that are advised to go through. These reflections go over impermanence (chapter 4), the suffering of *saṃsāra* (chapter 5), *karma* (chapter 6) love and compassion (chapter 7). Chapters 8 to 11 focus on the refuge and development of *bodhicitta*, then chapters 12-17 expand on the six *pāramitās* – generosity, ethics, patience, enthusiastic perseverance, enthusiasm, concentration, wisdom. The last chapters mention the different realizations on the path and describe awakening. This plan shows the extent to which the path is marked. Meditation is not a "random" practice, and awakening is not a mere coincidence, it has a well-defined methodology. Since the functioning of ordinary consciousness is identical for each human being, the means put into place to transform it are identical and applicable to all.

210 This is a *lam rim.* See Higgins 2012, note 552 p.219-220.

It is the *pāramitā* of wisdom which will take up most of our attention. The other practices and *pāramitās* are also important, since realizing emptiness cannot happen without them[211] - but they present fewer obstacles towards understanding. On the contrary, meditating on emptiness – specific to the *pāramitā* of wisdom – is less easy to grasp. Yet, it is the latter especially that will allow a better understanding of how to deconstruct the ordinary self, since only emptiness can uproot ignorance[212]. Besides, as J. O'Leary suggests, understanding more deeply the link between emptiness and liberation can also bring an interesting contribution compared to what has been written on the topic in the West:

> Deconstructing the ideas and the things, even pulverizing them through a skeptical analysis is a game that the philosophical mind has often conducted in the West. But this demystification has rarely been salutary. Yet, in the West, demonstrations of emptiness are twice as salutary, first in the sense that they take us closer to the dimension of the *nirvāṇa,* then in the sense that they set us free to uptake conventions again, in full consciousness of their fragility and constitutive inconsistency, so to say. O'Leary 2011, p.127-128.

As neither 3rd Karmapa nor Gampopa give precise enough meditation instructions about emptiness, we will primarily refer to another work of reference from the Kagyü lineage : ***Moonbeams of Mahāmudrā***[213] from Dakpo Tashi Namgyal (1512-1587). ***The Ocean of Definitive Meaning*** [214] of the 9th Karmapa Wangchouk Dorjé (1556-1603) is also a reference. The latter is a major work on the Mahāmudrā practice in the Karma Kagyü tradition. However, Dakpo Tashi Namgyal gives a lot more explanations and quo-

211 See the example of the paintors on the importance of each pāramita (RGV I.91-92/78-79). See also *Buddha Nature. The Mahāyāna Uttaratantra shastra with commentary* 2000, p.147; p.358; *The Jewel Ornement of Liberation,* p.233 and following ; *Moonbeams,* p.215-216.

212 *Moonbeams,* p.215-216. These ideas are also found in other texts, notably the MMK.

213 Tib. *nges don phyag rgya chen po'i sgom rim gsal bar bye dpa legs bshad zla ba'i 'od zer zhes bya ba bzhugs so.*

214 Tib. *phyag chen nges don rgya mtsho.*

tations than the 9th Karmapa[215]. According to transmissions from Kamtsang[216], the book of Dakpo Tashi Namgyal represents the Mahāmudrā sutras and the book of the 9th Karmapa represents the Essence Mahāmudrā[217]. This would explain why the first is way more detailed than the second.

Dakpo Tashi Namgyal presents the superior view in two steps primarily : "Determining the Essence of Mind, The root" [218], and " "Determining the Essence of Thoughts and Appearances, [Mind's] Expressive Power" [219]. These correspond to the emptiness of individual and the emptiness of phenomena. Other practices will also be convened and presented to elaborate on the deconstruction of the self.

Ordinary consciousness' particularity is to freeze or fix a certain image of itself and the world. This view constitutes its "self" – a hard and compact core that configurates and determines existence. Meditation's goal is to relax and open this "self" constructed by consciousness. With each turning, we will ask ourselves which cognitive change is observed consecutively with the meditation practice, how the change in perception allows the pacification of consciousness, and what is its principle of action.

First turning: Realization of the emptiness of personal self – the state of *arhat*

Meditation technique

Moonbeams

The first stage is the realization of self-emptiness. Several different reasonings demonstrate that there is no substantial self. The practitioner must observe and search amidst their experience whether what is discovered intellectually can be verified concretely. Dakpo

215 See Preface from Christian Charrier p. 18-20.

216 Kaṁ tshang.

217 Mathes 2008, p.44 (oral information from Ponlob Rinpoche).

218 *Moonbeams,* p.224.

219 *Moonbeams,* p.237.

Tashi Namgyal writes that to do so, it is thus necessary to search consciousness[220], observe with great care and profoundly what consciousness actually is.

It is essential to adopt an appropriate physical posture, because body and consciousness are intimately linked. It will be difficult to stabilize consciousness if the body is not positioned appropriately. The posture that is most advised and used is the posture in seven gestures[221]. Once settled, the practitioner is invited to settle their consciousness amidst quietness, then to look for the characteristics of consciousness – its aspect, its color, its shape[222], etc. Indeed, if a substantial self exists, specific characteristics or distinctive traits should be perceived - thus this idea to "search consciousness" by looking into whether the latter has a color or shape. If it exists intrinsically, something must be found somewhere, whether that is at the level of the body or at the level of consciousness, since the term consciousness must be understood through these two aspects[223]. The search must be continued until the practitioner is sure that it is not possible to find *a* consciousness.

> Mind must examine itself, like a rock pulverizing bones.
> *Moonbeams*, p.227.

The search must not stop until the practitioner is absolutely convinced that there is no self. It is important to have a lived experience for each question that is asked – answering "yes, there is no color or shape" can arise from a simple intellectual understanding or a brief glimpse. The answer must anchor itself in a certitude that one does not see anything such as a self. In order to test our understanding, honest conversations with the meditation master are essential[224].

---

220 Tib. *sems tshal.*

221 *Moonbeams,* p.180-182. The beneficial effects of each of these gestures on the subtle body and consciousness are described on page 182, as well as the negative effects of situations when physical posture is not appropriate.

222 It is difficult to distinguish between *gzugs* and *dbyibs*, which we translate here by "shape" in both cases.

223 NTC, Stanza 21.

224 *The Mahāmudrā: Eliminating the darkness of ignorance,* p.64-65.

These couple of explanations are clear, but perhaps too short. Since Dakpo Tashi Namgyal indicates that meditation on the essence of consciousness is comparable to the meditation on the personal self emptiness in the sūtras[225], another meditation technique will be studied in order to further describe the process of deconstructing the self.

Satipaṭṭhāna sutta

The meditative practices aimed at no self? and the associated realizations are not identical – different schools exist[226]. However, like other authors, the 3rd Karmapa does not make any distinction between them in the *Treatise on Pointing Out Buddha Nature.* He distinguishes only among the *arhats* the *śrāvakas*[227] and the *pratyekabouddhas*[228]. As for Jamgön Kongtrul Lodrö Thayé, he cites a couple of meditative practices related to the Hīnayāna in his commentary of stanza 48 – the mundane *samādhis* from the kingdom of form and formless; the four types of foundations of attention; the meditation of the twelve links in the reverse order[229] the eight liberations and the absorptive meditations. In the *Supreme Continuum*, an indication of practice of the *arhats* is also given:

> In brief, the fruit of these [purifying causes]
> fully divides into the remedies [for the antidotes],
> which [in their turn] counteract the four aspects
> of wrong beliefs with regard to the dharmakāya[230]. *Buddha Nature*, p.24.

"Children" or immature beings[231] have four erroneous views on

225 *Moonbeams*, p.226.

226 Cf. Swearer Donald K.,1987; Griffiths, 1999.

227 Tib. *nyan thos.*

228 Tib. *rang sangs rgyas*. NT, Stanza 41.

229 Generally attributed to the *pratyekabuddhas*.

230 *'di dag 'bras ni mdor bsdu na/ chos kyi sku la phyin ci log/ rnam pa bzhi las bzlog pa yi/ gnyen pos rab tu phye ba nyid/*

231 Tib. *byis ba*. The child designates the being that are still in illusion, in imagination. See

the nature of phenomena[232] : the impure phenomena are perceived as pure; suffering is seen as happiness; they grasp onto a self that does not exist; and impermanence is perceived as permanent. In order to eradicate these inaccurate views, the *arhats* cultivate on the contrary the perception of impurity (in particular that of the body), suffering, absence of self, and impermanence. These reflections allow one to gain perspective about what is mistaken as true.

It is not possible to know which realization and which practice(s) the 3rd Karmapa references points to. The term "*arhat*" seems especially used to characterize the first turning of the wheel. It would be impossible to examine all the previously mentioned practices – that is why only one of them will be retained: the four foundations of attention. Three reasons justify this choice. First of all, the instructions for this meditation described in the *Satipaṭṭhāna sutta* clearly show how to reach emptiness of self. Then, this practice corresponds to the first four factors of awakening exposed on the path to accumulation[233]. It therefore seems logical to start with this practice, since the latter marks the beginning of the path to Buddhahood. The last reason for this choice can be explained by the literature that is available on this topic. The work of Anālayo untitled *Satipaṭṭhāna: the direct path to realization*, includes an English translation of the *sutta* and a detailed and clear commentary[234]. Besides, Paul Griffiths suggests that this *sutta* is that which describes in the most simple and efficient ways the development of superior views[235].

It is always difficult to claim whether two practices lead to the same results. Dakpo Tashi Namgyal only wrote that « determining the essence of mind-itself is similar to determining the lack of a self of persons in the Sutra context »[236], which remains quite vague.

Scherrer Schaub, *Yuktiṣaṣṭikāvṛtti. Commentaire à la soixantaine sur le raisonnement ou Du vrai enseignement de la causalité par le maître indien Candrakīrti*, note 39, Bruxelles, Institut belge des hautes études chinoises (« Mélanges chinois et bouddhiques » 25), 1991.

232 *Buddha Nature. The Mahāyāna Uttaratantra shastra with commentary* 2000, p.123.

233 See NTC, Stanza 24; Cox. C. note 34 in Gyasto, 1992, p.94-95.

234 A French translation also exists in *L'enseignement du Bouddha. D'après les textes les plus anciens*, from Walopla Rahula, p.135-147. See also Thich Nath Hanh, *Transformation et guérison: Le sutra des quatre établissements de l'attention*, Albin Michel 1999.

235 Griffiths, *Concentration or insight: The Problematic of Theravāda Buddhist Meditation-Theory*, The Journal of the American Academy of Religion, XLIX/4, p.614, 1981.

236 *Moonbeams*, p.226.

Nevertheless, the study of *Satipaṭṭhāna Sutta* at least gives a more precise idea on the new habits to cultivate in order to dissolve grasping. Even if this meditation does not render the exact same fruit than that of the practice suggested in *Moonbeams,* it still offers a good starting point to understand the process of self-deconstruction.

Cognitive transformation

Four objects of attention to deconstruct the individual self

Satipaṭṭhāna is composed of *"sati"* – "attention" – and *"upaṭṭhāna"* – "to place oneself close to", which is to stay « being present to » [237]. The objects that one must be present to are the body, sensations, states of consciousness, and *dhammas*. The term « *dhamma* » designates the analyses of experience according to the categories of Buddhism, such as the obstacles, the factors of awakening, the Four Nobles Truths ...[238] It is easier to first start from the body because the latter is more tangible – it is therefore suggested first. The grosser experiences are set as beginning point, then the practitioner moves towards subtler experiences[239].

Some commentaries link every object of attention to one *skandha*[240]. The *skandhas* represent the five aggregates that constitute

237 Anālayo 2003 (2010), p.29-30.

238 Anālayo explains in pages 182-183 why« *dhammas* » cannot be translated by mental objects.

239 "On closer inspection, the sequence of the contemplations listed in the *Satipaṭṭhāna Sutta* reveals a progressive pattern. Contemplation of the body progresses from the rudimentary experience of bodily postures and activities to contemplating the body's anatomy. The increased sensitivity developed in this way forms the basis for contemplation of feelings, a shift of awareness from the immediately accessible physical aspects of experience to feelings as more refined and subtle objects of awareness. [...] Considered in this way, the sequence of the *satipaṭṭhāna* contemplation leads progressively from grosser to more subtle levels". Anālayo 2003 (2010), p.19-20.

240 Anālayo 2003 (2010), p.24.

the psycho-physical experience the form[241], sensations[242], notions, mental formations et consciousnesses[243]. The body would correspond to the *skandha* of forms, the sensations would correspond to the second *skandha*, the states of consciousness to the fifth, and the *dhammas* to the second and third (the notions et mental formations). The comparison is slightly forced since contemplation of states of consciousness includes all the mental elements, not only consciousness as it is described in the fifth *skandha*. Nevertheless, the goal is to show that these four objects of attention encompass the whole of subjective experience[244]. Each aggregate shows that everything can be decomposed in several elements that are interacting with one another, and none of them can take on the role of a self. This way, by bringing closer the objects of attention of the

---

241 « *Rūpa* » in sanscrit or « *gzugs* » in tibetan is sometimes translated by « matter », however this term is too limited compared to the elements that compose this whole. Indeed, matter is defined as a "substance from which perceived bodies are made of and whose fundamental characteristics are the area and mass" - "substance dont sont faits les corps perçus par les sens et dont les caractéristiques fondamentales sont l'étendue et la masse » (Trésor de la langue française). But this set also includes five types of mental objects that cannot be associated to matter. That is why the term of form is retained – it is more general and therefore more appropriate for this set. The form is a « set of characteristic traits that allow a concrete or abstract reality to be recognized » (Trésor de la langue française).

242 sct. *vedanā*, tib. *tshor ba*. Sensations are distributed in eighteen types. They can come from six consciousnesses and are either neutral, pleasant, or unpleasant – therefore there are eighteen types of possible sensations. Depending on what is perceived, the body feels pleasant or unpleasant sensations. By emphasizing sensations, the analysis of the *skandhas* shows that there is a link between body and consciousness: all sensory or mental perceptions have an impact at the level of the body.

243 The sensation can be also found in the *skandha* of mental formations. By putting it aside, we can hypothesize that the *Abhidharma* seeks to show the importance of sensation in the process of perceiving. Besides, this informs us that body and consciousness are related.

244 "According to the commentaries, each of the four *satipaṭṭhānas* corresponds to a particular aggregate: the aggregates of material form (*rūpa*), feeling (*vedanā*), and consciousness (*viññāṇa*) match the first three *satipaṭṭhānas*, while the aggregates of cognition (*saññā*) and volitions (*saṅkhārā*) correspond to the contemplation of *dhammas*. On closer inspection, this correlation appears a little forced, since the third *satipaṭṭhāna,* contemplation of mind, corresponds to all mental aggregates and not only to consciousness. Moreover, the fourth *satipaṭṭhāna,* contemplation of *dhammas*, includes the entire set of the five aggregates as one of its meditations, and thus has a wider range than just the two aggregates of cognition (*saññā*) and volition (*saṅkhārā*). Nevertheless, what the commentaries might intend to indicate is that all aspects of one's subjective experience are to be investigated with the aid of the four *satipaṭṭhānas*. Understood in this way, the division into four *satipaṭṭhānas* represents an analytical approach similar to a division of subjective experience into the five aggregates. Both attempts to dissolve the illusion of the observer's substantiality". Anālayo 2003 (2010), p.24.

skandhas, it is brought forward clearly that this practice aims to dissolve the illusion of a substantial self. The association of *skandhas* is therefore very didactic, because it establishes a direct link between theoretical analysis and meditation practice.

The practice of *Satipaṭṭhāna* gives more indications on the ways that we must look at our experience. The realization of no self is not only to see more clearly what is happening within our experience Indeed, even if we were way more attentive to the body, whether the latter was in movement or at rest, or even to different sensations, this would not interrupt our grasping to what manifests itself. The belief in a self and the three poisons would still be happening. It is not sufficient to place oneself above the body, sensations, states of consciousness and *dhammas* to recognize self-emptiness. This presence must be accompanied by mental qualities and specific trainings.

Qualities to cultivate[245]

> Here, monks, in regard to the body a monk abides contemplating[246] the body, diligent, clearly knowing, and mindful[247], free from desires and discontent in regard to the world. In regard to feelings he abides contemplating feelings, diligent, clearly knowing, and mindful, free from desires and discontent in regard to the world. In regard to the mind he abides contemplating the mind, diligent, clearly knowing, and mindful, free from desires and discontent in regard to the world. In regard to *dhammas* he abides contemplating *dhammas,* diligent, clearly knowing, and mindful, free from desires and discontent in regard to the world. Anālayo 2003 (2010), p.3-4.

245 For an explanation of each of these qualities, see Anālayo 2003 (2010), chapters 2, 3 et 4. *Sati* is the most important quality to develop – however the *Buddha* declared in the *Maṇibhadda Sutta* that it cannot uproot by itself ill will (Anālayo 2003 (2010), p.52). Other qualities are necessary: seeing repeatedly, enthusiastic assiduity, clear seeing, and being free from desire and dissatisfaction.

246 Pāli.*anupassati.*

247 Pāli. *sati*

First of all, the observation must be repeated[248]. As soon as the observed object is lost, one must come back to it, again and again. The practitioner must also develop persistence or enthusiastic assiduity[249] in order to maintain the motivation to practice over time. Perseverance lies between effort and non-effort. It is necessary but should not be a source of tension either. The third quality is clear seeing[250]. The observation should not be superficial, but completely conscious of what manifests itself. Finally, the other quality that must accompany *sati* is to be free of all desire or dissatisfaction[251]. It is necessary to be free from hope and fear – which is to say the eight mundane *dharmas* – in order to be able to firmly establish oneself in meditation. If consciousness continues to be preoccupied by this or that thing, it will not be able to make any progress.

Sati - attention – is the first quality to cultivate[252]. The name "*sati*" is related to the verb sarati "to remember." In the sutta, it is not about remembering the past but being conscious of the present moment. It is thanks to sati that we can be in the present moment, that we can land on that is here now[253]. What is more, the different illustrations associated with sati reveal other characteristics: calm and detached observation, preliminary condition to wisdom, vigilance[254]. Attention is first and foremost naked observation, in the sense that it does not implicate any action on the consciousness

248 Pāli. *anupassati* : « *Passati* » means « to see» et le préfixe « *anu* » intensifies the verb. « *Anupassati* » can therefore be translated by « seeing repeatedly » or « see from very close », Anālayo 2003 (2010) p.32.

249 Pāli. *ātāpī.*

250 Pāli. *sampajāna*.

251 Pāli. *vineyya abhijjhādomanassa*.

252 On this subject, see Gyatso, 1992 (in particular the introduction and the article from C. Cox).

253 "The noun *sati* is related to the verb *sarati*, to remember. *Sati* in the sense of "memory" occurs on several occasions in the discourses, and also in the standard definitions of *sati* given in the *Abhidhamma* and the commentaries. [...] A closer examination of this definition, however, reveals that *sati* is not really defined as memory, but as that which facilitates and enables memory. What this definition of *sati* points to is that, it *sati* is present, memory will be able to function well. Understanding *sati* in this way facilitates relating it to the context of *satipaṭṭhāna,* where it is not concerned with recalling past events, but functions as awareness of the present moment. In this context of *satipaṭṭhāna* meditation, it is due to the presence of *sati* that one is able to remember what is otherwise only too easily forgotten: the present moment". Anālayo 2003 (2010), p.46-48.

254 See Anālayo 2003 (2010), p.53-57; 122.

or the body, it only observes what it manifests[255]. The attention observes, it does not seek to suppress psychic or physical elements, or to change the content of experience – only being conscious of what is manifesting itself [256]. « *Sati* » encompasses an attention that does not do[257].

There is no action strictly speaking, and yet experience deepens[258]. Indeed, the observation allows to see how the reactions start and which configurations underly them.

> As soon as one becomes in any way involved in a reaction, the detached observational vantage point is immediately lost. The detached receptivity of sati enables one to step back from the situation at hand and thereby to become an unbiased observer of one's subjective involvement and of the entire situation. Dhīravaṃsa, 1988, p.31[259].

---

255 "A close examination of the instructions in the *Satipaṭṭhāna Sutta* reveals that the meditator is never instructed to interfere actively with what happens in the mind. If a mental hindrance arises, for example, the task of *satipaṭṭhāna* contemplation is to know that the hindrance is present, to know what has led to its arising, and to know what will lead to its disappearance. A more active intervention is no longer the domain of *satipaṭṭhāna*, but belongs rather to the province of right effort (*sammā vāyāna*).
The need to distinguish clearly between a first stage of observation and a second stage of action taking is, according to the Buddha, an essential feature of his way of teaching. The simple reason for this approach is that only the preliminary step of calmly assessing a situation without immediately reacting enables one to undertake the appropriate action. *Sati* can interact with other, much more active factors of the mind, yet by itself it does not interfere". Anālayo 2003 (2010), p.57.

256 "Uninvolved and detached receptivity as one of the crucial characteristics of *sati* forms an important aspect in the teachings of several modern meditation teachers and scholars. They emphasize that the purpose of *sati* is solely to make things conscious, not to eliminate them. *Sati* silently observe, like a spectator at a play, without in any way interfering". Anālayo 2003 (2010), p.58.

257 "*Sati* as a mental quality is closely related to attention (manasikāra), a basic function which, according to the *Abhidhammic* analysis, is present in any kind of mental state. This basic faculty of ordinary attention characterizes the initial split seconds of bare cognizing of an object, before one begins to recognize, identify, and conceptualize. *Sati* can be understood as a further development and temporal extension of this type of attention, thereby adding clarity and depth to the usually much too short fraction of time occupied by bare attention in the perceptual process". Anālayo 2003 (2010), p.59.

258 That is, *sati* does not change experience, it deepens it". Anālayo 2003 (2010), p.58.

259 Cited in Anālayo 2003 (2010), p. 58.

"Naked attention" thus has the power to lead a de-automatization of mental mechanisms[260]. It then becomes possible to see without projection, and consciousness can develop new cognitive habits that are less and less attached to *saṃskāras*[261].

The refrain

> In this way, in regard to the body he abides contemplating the body internally, or he abides contemplating the body externally, or he abides contemplating the body both internally and externally. He abides contemplating the nature of arising in the body, or he abides contemplating the nature of passing away in the body, or he abides contemplating the nature of both arising and passing away in the body. Mindfulness that « there is a body » is established in him to the extent necessary for bare knowledge and continous mindfulness. And he abides independent, not clinging to anything in the world. Anālayo 2003 (2010), p.3-4.

After defining the qualities of consciousness that are to be developed and the four objects on which attention is established, the "refrain" [262] must also be applied. What was previously mentioned is not sufficient to the in-depth transformation of consciousness's mechanisms. Indeed, only the foundations to develop a clarity of experience have been established. A refrain is therefore repeated after each object that attention went to; it gives the "modus operandi" leading to a superior vision[263].

260 "This "bare attention" aspect of *sati* has an intriguing potential, since it is capable of leading to a "de-automatization" of mental mechanisms. Through bare *sati* one is able to see things just as they are, unadulterated by habitual reactions and projections. By bringing the perceptual process into full light of awareness, one becomes conscious of automatic and habitual responses to perceptual data Full awareness of these automatic responses is the necessary preliminary step to changing detrimental mental habits". Anālayo 2003 (2010), p.60.

261 In chapters 6 and 13 of the work of Anālayo, the benefits of the practice for each of the objects of attention are described.

262 Anālayo 2003 (2010), Chapter 5.

263 « Throughout the discourse, a particular formula follows each individual meditation prac-

First, the refrain suggests meditating on internal phenomena and also external ones. Internal phenomena pertain to subjective experience. Once better understood, the *sutta* invites the practitioner to observe others' experience. Does these same phenomena happen for other people? Are the discoveries in my body and consciousness verified through others' experience? Then, observing appearance and disappearance is advised[264]. In other words, this is a meditation on impermanence. The third instruction of the refrain is bare knowledge, which is to say a knowledge that does not get lost in different associations and reactions, and a continued attention[265]. The practice must be done continuously because only continuity can change habits[266]. Finally, the last thing to practice is independence or absence of attachment[267]. If desire, rejection, and indifference are pursued, consciousness identifies itself and no clarity can arise. A bare knowledge without the three poisons is equivalent to the practice of equanimity.

Putting the refrain in practice seems determinant for the realization of no-self. Indeed, the realization of impermanence of everything that constitutes experience is a key point to see that there is no substantial "me." Everything is always in movement, "I" is continually transforming. A special interaction between body and consciousness happens and changes in each instant[268].

For the realization of the no-self to be total, cultivating equanimity is also necessary. Indeed, the idea of the self is fed by the three poisons. By developing equanimity, which is to say by not being carried away by the mechanisms of adoption and rejection,

---

tice. This *satipaṭṭhāna* « refrain » completes each instruction by repeatedly emphasizing the important aspects of the practice. Note 9: The fact that this "refrain" is indispensable to each meditation exercise is shown by the remark concluding each occurrence of the "refrain"." Analayo 2003 (2010), p.18.

264 Anālayo 2003 (2010), p.102-107.

265 Pāli. *ñāṇamattāya paṭissatimattāya*.

266 Anālayo 2003 (2010), p.93 and cf. explications of *sati*.

267 Pāli. *anissito ca viharati, na ca kiñci loke upādiyati*. Anālayo 2003 (2010), p.112-116.

268 "Continuity in developing awareness of impermanence is essential if it is really to affect one's mental condition. Sustained contemplation of impermanence leads to a shift in one's normal way of experiencing reality, which hitherto tacitly assumed the temporal stability of the perceiver and the perceived objects. Once both are experienced as changing processes, all notions of stable existence and substantially vanish, thereby radically reshaping one's paradigm of experience. See Anālayo 2003 (2010), p.105.

there will be no more grasping on what appears. The three poisons cannot arise since equanimity is their contrary. The practice of the *Satipaṭṭhāna sutta* therefore allows to realize, which is to say to see directly, the absence of a self[269]. Besides, the practice shows that meditation is not a work on the contents of experience but on the mechanisms of experience. It is this type of understanding that results in a superior vision[270]. The self that seemed so dense dilates and appears in a new light – it is constituted of different elements which interact with each other[271].

The peace of the individual emptiness

The realization of the no-self allows access to *nirvāṇa*[272], to peace. *Nirvāṇa* is often compared to the extinction of a lamp or a fire, because the metaphor of the quenched fire in ancient India often evokes calm, independence, liberation[273]. Walpola Rahula also uses a citation in which the image of the quenched flame is used to show what *nirvāṇa* is:

269 We will later return on the instruction that consists of observing internal and external phenomena.

270 "This shift of awareness from the individual content of a particular experience to its general features is of central importance for the development of insight. Here the task of *sati* is to penetrate beyond the surface appearance of the object under observation and to lay bare the characteristics it shares with all conditioned phenomena. This move of *sati* towards the more general characteristics of experience brings about insight into the impermanent, unsatisfactory, and selfless nature of reality. Such a more panoramic kind of awareness emerges at an advanced stage of *satipaṭṭhāna,* once the meditator is able to maintain awareness effortlessly". Anālayo 2003 (2010), p.93-94.

271 This conclusion can be linked with the commentary from Jamgön Kongtrul Lodrö Thayé in stanza 4 : "[...] except for the illusionary tendencies of ignorance, what we call "ordinary being" does not exist beforehand either." NTC, Stanza 4, our translation (see also Brunnhölzl 2009, p.209). Emptiness reveals another form of "being." The term "ordinary being" does not have an ontological meaning, it points to an aggregate of ignorant tendencies. Numerous studies have been conducted on the no-self, for example: Steven Collins, *Selfless Persons: Imagery and Thought in Theravada Buddhism*, Cambridge University Press, 2009; Mark Siderits, *Personal identity and Buddhist philosophy: empty persons*, Aldershot (England Burlington VT) : Ashgate, 2003.

272 Pāli. *nibbāna.*

273 Anālayo 2003 (2010), p.257.

> As he does not construct or does not will continuity and becoming or annihilation, he does not cling to anything in the world; as he does not cling, he is not anxious; as he is not anxious, he is completely calmed within (fully blown out within paccattamyeva parinibbayati). Rahula 1978 p.39.

Thanks to the attention that brings consciousness back into the present moment and into the body, consciousness is at rest. Indeed, not being caught in the different thoughts about the past or future is a source of appeasement. Additionally, while in pain, if consciousness does not get lost in the different discourses about what it feels, the pain will have a different flavor. Thinking about pain, naming it, complaining about it, or even worrying about what will happen next are features that can generate anxiety and keep the subject away from what they are feeling. In the contrary, applying what is described in the *sutta* brings consciousness in contact with experience itself, with equanimity[274].

The realization of impermanence also deeply changes mental habits. As soon as there is no more identification to a "self," no more grasping, the internal space expands and, in doing so, becomes able to welcome what presents itself with fewer tensions. At the level of the ordinary, a certain reading grid of the world that is quite fixed is in place. If something happens and does not align with our beliefs, the capacity to accept and adapt shrinks or even vanishes. By understanding the concept of impermanence and equanimity, consciousness improves and expands its capacity to face the world with more flexibility. Tolerance to "cognitive dissonance" increases:

> Maintaining the presence of sati in this way is closely related to the ability to tolerate a high degree of « cognitive dissonance », since the witnessing of one's own

274 It is also interesting to follow the multiplication of scientific studies on the effects of meditation, especially in relation the Mindfulness-Based Stress Reduction protocol (MBSR), which is founded on the principle of *sati*. The following article, although slightly dated, offers a good overview: Guido Bondolfi, *Les approches utilisant des exercices de méditation de type «mindfulness» ont-elles un rôle à jouer?,* Santé mentale au Québec, vol. 29, n° 1, 2004, p. 137-145.

> shortcomings ordinarily leads to unconscious attempts at reducing the resulting feeling of discomfort by avoiding or even altering the perceived information[275]. Anālayo 2003 (2010), p. 59.

Consciousness understands the mechanisms that lead to dissatisfaction, it is then able to free itself from them and is not chained to the wheel of *saṃsāra* anymore.

Action

At the level of the ordinary, actions are directed by the three poisons. The three poisons form the desire to act of non-awakened beings. How does the *arhat* conducts their actions if they are not moved anymore by this principle? Since the three poisons are causes of suffering – the second Noble Truth even claims that desire is at the origin of suffering –it would be tempting to think that the *arhat* does not have any more desire since it is liberated from the *saṃsāra*. But if this is the case, then action would not be possible since every one of our acts is motivated by a desire. Let's remember that it is not desire in itself that is called into question, but desire founded on the idea of a substantial self[276]. Desire and ignorance must be taken together to understand what is truly problematic with desire[277]. Therefore, self-liberation is not a suppression of the desiring consciousness, self-liberation of self is neither a negation of life nor the absence of emotions. In reality, the dissolution of the three poisons leads to another form of action.

Strictly speaking, ordinary action is more a reaction than an action, as it is strongly determined by *saṃskāras*, our conditioning. Observing what arises in a bare way and with equanimity allows the pacification of the process. The application of *sati* and of the

275 This term points to the theory developed by Léon Festinger in *A theory of cognitive dissonance* (1957).

276 Perhaps this is the reason why the Mahāyāna rather insists on ignorance as a source of illusion.

277 This is confirmed with the Wheel of Life whose twelve links are in conditioned coproduction – we find ignorance and desire on the first and seventh links respectively. Besides, it is said that desire is a cause of suffering. Desire, or thirst, is neither the first nor the unique cause of *dukkha*'s appearance, but it is its most palpable and immediate source.

refrain dismantle such process by coming back to the sources of the mental activity that drive action before any identification or conceptualization. Before, the significations were evident, with practice, everything unfolds like a reading in slow motion. Consciousness is able to perceive the different steps that lead to this or that signification, and thanks to this vision or detachment, it can change what is harmful to its own mental and physical well-being. In addition, in the refrain of the *sutta*, meditating on internal phenomena but also external is suggested. The internal phenomena are about subjective experience, once the latter is better understood, the practitioner is invited to observe others' experience. Are the discoveries made within my body and consciousness verified in others? By observing that others' reactions are caused by similar mechanisms to ours, our tendency towards rejection, revolt, or harmful actions quenches. Indeed, why becoming angry towards someone who is locked into ignorance, who does not recognize the different interactions in the game? That is what Śāntideva writes in chapter 6 (on patience) in *A Guide to the Bodhisattva's Way of Life:*

> 22. As I do not become angry
> With great sources of suffering such as jaundice,
> Then why be angry with animate creatures?
> They too are provoked by conditions.
>
> 33. So when seeing an enemy or even a friend
> Committing an improper action,
> By thinking that such things arise from conditions
> I shall remain in a happy frame of mind[278].

Therefore, this knowledge at least plays the role of shock-absorber. We are less often plunged in incomprehension, wondering what is going on. This prevents us from over-reacting or getting carried

278 Śāntideva, A Guide to the Bodhisattva's Way of Life, translated by Stephen Batchelor, p.47 ; 49. https://www.tibethouse.jp/about/buddhism/text/pdfs/Bodhisattvas_way_English.pdf

away[279]. The acts that are so-called "negative" diminish. Besides, the realization of the no-self implies the absence of the three poisons, the absence of an image to defend at any cost. When there is nothing to defend, it is much easier to be open to others. Charles Goodman takes the example of national identity to show how the realization of a no-self can lead to compassion. If we define our identity as radical Serbian nationalism, we will perceive the other as Croatian. Hence, we will be insensitive to their suffering. But if we see the absurdity of holding onto Serbian nationalism, or any other view as the absolute truth, we will perceive others' suffering and will naturally want to diminish it[280]. It is even indicated that action can become spontaneously virtuous[281]. And yet, can we still talk about kindness?

Kindness is an affective disposition that aims for the good and happiness of others. The link therefore does not appear clearly at this stage. Kindness towards oneself develops and must develop itself to obtain a result, but other practices seem necessary to orient consciousness towards the accomplishment of others' benefit. Some sūtras invite the practitioner to develop for example the four illimited qualities - love, compassion, joy, and equanimity[282]. It is also common that a meditation on love and kindness will be offered after a practice[283], this allows the giving of a direction, a destination.

Even if the sole practice of attention is not sufficient to develop kindness, it is encouraged, and it remains an essential foundation so that the actions for others' benefit remain authentic.

How to understand in this case the reason by which Rangjung Dorje describes the *arhats'* peace as personal, like an extreme to be avoided[284] ?

Limits

The 3rd Karmapa Rangjung Dorje considers that the realization of

279 Can also be explained by less negative thoughts, no image to defend (example of Goodman).

280 Goodman 2009, p.50.

281 Anālayo 2003 (2010), p.258.

282 Keown 1992.

283 Charles Goodman 2009, p.49-50; Peter Harvey 2000, p.103-109.

284 « [Awakening] is not similar to the peace of the śrāvakas and the pratyekabouddhas ». NT, Stanza 41 [192], and NT, Stanza 48.

arhats is less advanced than that of *buddhas.* The arhat's limits are first cognitive, which will necessarily have an influence on the peace that is reached and the mode of action.

Cognitive limits

Thanks to the practice exposed in the *Satipaṭṭhāna sutta,* the arhat realizes the individual emptiness. One's view on experience is clearer, less substantial. The *arhat* sees the links between the body and consciousness – they acquire a mastery on what arises, they do not get carried away anymore by *saṃskāras*. The arhat reaches this stage thanks to the application of remedies. In the *Satipaṭṭhāna sutta,* it is primarily a question of sati, of equanimity and impermanence. Sati and equanimity allow one not to react to what is perceived, but rather to create more space in order to be in greater adequation with the situation. Impermanence is a reminder that nothing lasts eternally, everything ends up passing, and impermanence is lived, experienced. Other remedies often attributed to *arhats* also consist in avoiding that the perceived object be a source of vagrancy. For example, it is advised to cultivate a vision of the body's impurity if the desire for another's body arises, or to remind oneself that the saṃsāra is only suffering. The principle every time is to replace the content of the perceived object or to adopt an attitude that prevents one from being absorbed by the object. It is precisely this principle that allows the characterization of the limit of the *arhat*'s realization. Let's take the example of the remedy to the body's impurity. Ordinary beings think that the body is desirable because it can be a source of pleasures. If they develop attachment towards physical pleasures, different afflictions can arise. To remedy this situation, cultivating the thought of the body's impurity diminishes the attraction towards such body, since instead of seeing the body as source of pleasures, it will be seen as an aggregate composed of bones, blood, pus, nails, etc. The thought about impurity is therefore a remedy. However, the body's impurity can become a new truth or a new attachment. The body's impurity therefore becomes a new reference on which consciousness founds itself. The representation of the body changed, but the problem is that the body is still a representation. Indeed, the notions of purity and impurity are the result of thoughts, there is no more basis to impurity than there is of purity, and this reasoning can be applied to remedies as well. Every time, there is a new mental representation that prevents a direct recognition of what is. This new configuration is perhaps more in adequation with the real, but it still belongs to grasping. By applying these remedies, the *arhat* does not recognize the true nature of their experience, and they stay still in the body-consciousness-thought framework. The *arhat* is more into peace but always with references. In other words, this practice still leaves behind the subject of experience, it stays separate, facing a world that resists it.

This explanation can also be applied to the instructions offered in the *Satipaṭṭhāna sutta*. However, understanding how impermanence, equanimity, and attention are cognitive limits is less obvious, since these three factors do not seem to be representations. Let's start with impermanence. Ordinary consciousness perceives time in gross manners – time is almost still, and linear. Consciousness evolves along a line marked by past, present, and future. The *arhat*, thanks to meditation on impermanence, entertains another relationship with time since they are sensitive to changes, and they are more often into the present moment. They are conscious of the dynamic of consciousness and body sensations. Time is not fixed anymore, it recovers a certain fluidity, and their consciousness is less dispersed between past and future. Indeed, in order to be conscious of movement, one must be in the present moment. However, being in the present moment does not necessarily implies being freed up from linearity. It is absolutely possible to be in a present moment that is distorted by the past and oppressed by perspectives of the future. Even if consciousness comes closer to the present moment, the latter might not be completely open, in the sense that past and future are following it closely. We always go from a point A to a point B, along a path that is set by *saṃskāras*. Thus, even if the experience is much more flexible, more relaxed, it moves along a line. The "vital time," which is to say the life of the body and consciousness, is felt – psychological time mislays consciousness less often because the latter has a better capacity to stay in the present moment, but a dimension of time that escapes us still remains. Time, in its "pure state" must be free from any mental elaboration[285], which is to say any form of representations, as we will later see. As for attention and equanimity, they are used to defuse reactions and make consciousness clearer. But what is the depth of the lived experience of the body? Are all of consciousness's faculties discovered? How about internal/external duality?

Rangjung Dorje writes in stanza 6 that *nirvāṇa* [personnal] has ignorance as soil. The causes of saṃsāra are the inauthentic formations and the causes of *nirvāṇa* are the authentic formations or remedies. Thus, the previous remedies still pertain from a type of ignorance, and it is possible to go further thanks to the recognition of *dharmakāya* :

> In brief, the fruit of these [purifying causes]
> fully divides into the remedies [for the antidotes],
> which [in their turn] counteract the four aspects
> of wrong beliefs with regard to the dharmakāya.
>
> The [dharmakāya] is purity, since its nature is pure
> and [even] the remaining imprints are fully removed.
> It is true self, since all conceptual elaboration
> in terms of self and non-self is totally stilled.
> It is true happiness, since [even] the aggregates
> of mental nature and their causes are reversed.
> It is permanence, since the cycle of existence
> and the state beyond pain are realized as one. *Buddha Nature,* p.24.

In this excerpt, the *dharmakāya* is associated with purity, permanence, bliss, and a self. This description is not a matter of chance, but it echoes the four remedies cultivated by the arhat. By claiming that the *dharmakāya* is permanent, a self, bliss and pure, the author suggests that the arhats's antidotes must not be taken as new references. One must go beyond the ideas of purity and impurity, of self and no-self, of bliss and suffering, of permanence and imper-

285 Sct. *niṣprapañca*, tib. *spros bral.*

manence[286]. This state corresponds to the absence of mental elaborations. That is why from the standpoint of the *dharmakāya*, the antidotes of the *arhat* are distorsions[287]. They are useful to remedy to false beliefs, but one must also go beyond them. These dichotomies can be beneficial on the path when the practitioner is under the influence of afflictions, but after arriving to this stage, they must go beyond all duality. The choice of these four qualifiers of *dharmakāya* is therefore another remedy to eradicate grasping that is less gross –and not a "step backward."

Limited Peace and Action

This cognitive limitation also has an impact on the *arhat's level of peace and activity*. Rangjung Dorje mentions in the *Treatise Pointing Out Buddha Nature* that *arhats* are not in supreme peace[288]. Consequently, *arhats* are also immersed in a form of suffering that must be differentiated from that of ordinary beings. *Arhats* become aware of ordinary consciousness's functioning, and, in this way, do not let themselves get carried away in the spiral of *saṃsāra*. Thanks to their meditative practice, afflictions and *karma* dwindle. Yet, the *arhat's* peace is not total, because according to the *Supreme Continuum*, the *arhat* fears the suffering of the *saṃsāra*. What is more, even if the action of the *arhat* is more beneficial than that of ordinary beings, it nevertheless remains limited because they have not developed universal love:

> Enmity towards the Dharma, a view [asserting an existing] self,
> fear of samsara's suffering,
> and neglect of the welfare of fellow beings

---

286 We find here a process that seems similar to that which is used in the tantras, for example when the five meats and the five ambrosias are mentioned. See chapter 4 of the book from Christian K. Wedemeyer, *Making sense of Tantric Buddhism: History, Semiology and Transgression in the Indian traditions,* Columbia University Press, 2013. Besides, David Higgins devotes a section on the difference between "pure consciousness" and "nature of consciousness," Higgins 2012, p.78-82.

287 Tib. *phyin ci log.*

288 NT, Stanza 41.

> are the four veils of those with great desire,
> of *tīrthikas,* śrāvakas, and *pratyekabuddhas. Buddha Nature,* p.23-24.

This fear of *saṃsāra* and this lack of consideration for others can be explained by the presence of duality amidst the realization of the *arhat.* The remedies practiced at this point mainly pertain to the individual self. However, the self of phenomena is not subject to specific exercises. The world that the ordinary state perceives as external remains external for the *arhats,* whereas everything is only the reflection of consciousness from the standpoint of the Great Vehicle. The arhat eradicates the veils of affliction thanks to their understanding of no-self, but the latter does not purify all of the veils of the knowledgeable. Indeed, ignorance is not limited to self-grasping, it extends to all phenomena. Additionally, the arhat has meditated on the suffering of the *saṃsāra,* and there is an opposition between *saṃsāra* and *nirvāṇa.* This would explain why the *arhat* prefers to retreat in a peace which Rangjung Dorje qualifies as extreme, a peace withdrawn from the world, a peace that is afraid of the world.

Meditating on the suffering of *saṃsāra* does not encourage one to get involved for the benefit of others. From the standpoint of the *arhat* and particularly of the *pratyekabuddha,* being with others is an obstacle on the path, a distraction. Besides, since the saṃsāra is endless, why bother getting involved? This is not complete indifference, since the arhat develops love and compassion, but these qualities are not as vast as that of a buddha. The arhat is first and foremost concerned with their own salvation, their main worry is to free themselves from the cycle of rebirths, to stop coming back after death. "Personal peace" cannot designate an absence of love, but rather can indicate partial love because of a cognitive limitation, which, as we will, see, translates into an absence of means to support others. In other words, love and compassion can be much vaster and therefore even more beneficial.

Conclusion

Ordinary consciousness tends to perceive body and consciousness as two distinct entities with specific characteristics, thus giving the impression of a unique identity. Such consciousness is passive to its own experience because it always finds itself within the context of a certain signification, in a subject-object duality, without knowing how it got there. Thanks to the described practices, it is possible to re-appropriate our own experience is a much more precise way. Instead of being absorbed by mental habits, we are invited to explore our experience. Getting back in touch with the body, sensations... allows us to recover a certain richness of experience that dualistic grasping had repressed until then, and to see that the "self" is perhaps not what we thought it to be[289].

The vision can be deepened thanks to the realization of the emptiness of all phenomena[290]. The next meditative step thus involves "working" on the forms that still imprison consciousness, looking at them more closely in order to dissolve any separation between the subject and the world, being more present and more active within the experience without going back into the logic of the three poisons. After mind-body integration, internal-external duality is now examined. Consciousness must free itself up from any mental elaborations. Indeed, the main difference between the realization of an *arhat* and that of a buddha can be measured through the absence of these elaborations. Complete and perfect awakening challenges all forms of thoughts that are oriented by a certain structure, whether or not these are turning towards awakening[291]. The *arhats* have eliminated the veils of afflictions only – and the *bodhisattvas* progressively eradicate cognitive veils in the ten bhūmis until they attain perfect Buddhahood, where the two types of veils are completely abandoned, allowing a deeper and vaster peace.

---

289 "By turning awareness to different facets of one's subjective experience, these aspects will be experienced simply as objects, and the notion of compactness, the sense of a solid "I", will begin to disintegrate. In this way, the more subjective experience can be seen "objectively", the more the "I"-dentification diminishes. This correlates well with the Buddha's instruction to investigate thoroughly each aggregate to the point where no more "I" can be found". Anālayo 2003 (2010), p.24.

290 See Benefits and limits of individual emptiness.

291 We can find again this idea of a « structure-oriented way of thinking » in the work of Guenther, *From reductionism to creativity. rDzogs chen and the new sciences of Mind,* for example p.61;68.

Second Turning and the no-self of phenomena: intellectual understanding of emptiness

Emptiness aims to "eradicate all views," to recognize the true nature of phenomena that are completely free from any point of reference[292] :

> I prostrate to Gautama
> Who through compassion
> Taught the true doctrine,
> Which leads to the relinquishing of all views.[293] MMK, 27.30

> The victorious ones have said
> That emptiness is the relinquishing of all views[294]. MMK, 13.8

It is also pointed out that phenomena are "unborn" or "without beginning":

> It has been declared in [*the Abhidharmasūtra*]: "without beginning"
> Consequently, absolutely nothing exists beforehand. NT, Stanza 4 [13-14].

Any idea of beginning or end is an illusion. From an absolute standpoint, there is no foundation, which is why all phenomena are unborn, without beginning[295].

Different reasonings

292 Brunnhölzl 2009, p.88-89.

293 Garfiled 1995, p.352.

294 Garfiled 1995, p.212.

295 « The time of saṃsāra and nirvāṇa appearing and being mistaken as two is this very moment, it does not come via some place else, because all phenomena are dependent origination », NTC Stanza 4 in *Luminous Heart* p.209.

The second turning consists in "listening and thinking"[296], understanding emptiness intellectually.

In stanza 12, the 3rd Karmapa evokes the argument of neither one nor many[297], which is one of five reasonings that Madhyamaka uses to show the emptiness of all phenomena[298]. This reasoning aims to show that the belief in a substantial self always leads to logical incoherence, or an impossibility of empirical verification[299]. Any assertion of a theory in which a substantial self is at stake implies paradoxes. Ordinary logic and language therefore end up unfounded. Let's note that the 3rd Karmapa also evokes in stanza 11 a theory that is closer to the Yogācāra, which also proposed several arguments in order to challenge ordinary perception[300].

Whichever reasoning is used, the conclusion is always the same – it is not possible to find a foundation to what we think is true in itself. By observing our experience or basing our reasoning on logic, we find no foundation – the "self" is only the product of consciousness[301]. The thoughts, afflictions, different characteristics

---

296 NT, stanza 12. Besides, the 3rd Karmapa mentions these different forms of learning in the *Treatise on the Distinction between Consciousness and Wisdom* (NY [1-4]) or also in the *Aspiration Prayer of Mahāmudrā* (stanza 5). Dakpo Tashi Namgyal also uses this idea in *Moonbeams* (p.216-218). The view that is born from both study and reflection facilitates the development of a superior view. Study, reflection, and meditation do not perfectly correspond to the succession of the three turnings since study and reflection should take place even before meditation on the individual no-self.

297 Śāntarakṣita bases this argument on *Madhyamakālaṅkāra* (tib. *dbu ma rgyan*). See Tillemans, 1983, 1984; Blumenthal, 2009; Westerhoff, 2009 p.36-38 ; Kapstein 2001 ; Kellner & Taber 2014.

298 The Tibetan tradition summarized the arguments related to the Madhyamaka in five types of reasoning – the analysis of the cause of phenomena, called the reasoning of the « vajra droplets » (tib. *rdo rje gzegs ma*); "refuting the arising of something already existent or nonexistent" (tib. *yod med skye 'gog*); the analysis of the "refuting the four possibilities of arising" (tib. *mu bzhi skye 'gog*); "neither one nor many" (tib. *gcig dang du bral*); and the king of all reasonings, the analysis of "dependent arising" (tib. *rten 'brel*). For more details, see Brunnhölzl, 2004, pp. 231-264.

299 Bugault 1994, p.221-225.

300 For a more extensive explanation, it is suitable to look into the Indian texts of the Yogācāra. B. Chaterjee in his work *The Yogācāra Idealism* makes an inventory of the different arguments intended to refute the idea of realism (chapter 3 and 4) ; see also Brunnhölzl 2009, *Introduction* p.1-124.

301 Guy Bugault explains that "the dialectic of Nāgārjuna expands in reference to a double criteria: the comprehensibility of the terms, their positivity" (*L'Inde pense-t-elle ?* p.221). Nāgārjuna shows the inconsistency of a theory either by showing that there is no logical coherence, either by showing that the theory is denied by experience, or even by showing

attributed to objects are very real, in the sense that they show up to consciousness and are efficient, but they are not truly real, in the sense that they have no absolute foundation.

The paradoxes shed into light by the different arguments proposed allow for the making of a dent. Indeed, if our usual mode of knowing turns out to be unfounded, then why attach to it so much? The paradoxes put us at a distance from what usually absorbs us, they inaugurate a process of disidentification. The conventionality of our world is emphasized, and as a result, consciousness detaches from it, it puts it at a distance:

> Demonstrations of emptiness are salutary in two ways – first, they bring us closer to the dimension of *nirvāṇa*; then, they free us to take up conventions again, with full consciousness of their fragility and constitutive inconsistency, so to speak. O'Leary 2011, p.127-128.

One of the core benefits of the logical analysis is this beginning of detachment from views, to thoughts. The grasping of *saṃskāras, in other words all of our points of reference, weakens, thus facilitating a decrease in afflictions and a better perception of the real. This has already been possible with the practice of the Satipaṭṭhāna sutta, the intellectual understanding of emptiness probably strengthens this process and should lead us further down the path.*

Authentic imagination – a factor for awakening

Rangjung Dorje wrote that the beginning and end of *saṃsāra* is based on nothing else than imagination[302]. When imagination contributes to the perpetuation of *saṃsāra*, it is called inauthentic imagination; when imagination contributes to the end of *saṃsāra*, it is called authentic imagination[303]. Therefore, even if the absolute is inaccessible to the intellect, it is possible to resort to imagination

that there is no referent behind the words that are employed. In each case, the reasonings of the Madhyamaka confront us to paradoxes – everything that we think is founded on reality actually is not.

302 NT, Stanza 10 [33].

303 Or antidote thought (tib. *gnyen po'i rtogs*). The reflection must act like "anti-projections" (see *Beacon of Certainty* 4.18, translation Pettit 1999).

to prepare for awakening. Even if thinking about an ineffable topic seems paradoxical, it is in the end the only possible option. The only alternative is to work with tools that ordinary consciousness can understand in order to open the gate towards true transformation, towards another mode of knowing. Consciousness being the origin of both *saṃsāra* and *nirvāṇa,* at one point in the sequence of instants of knowing, there is a stage that makes us tip towards one or the other. In order to access *nirvāṇa,* we must therefore understand saṃsāra. Since ordinary consciousness can only evolve at first in a language that is its own, it is useful to first use means that resembles it.

Let's note that some texts from other traditions or philosophical schools display analyses that are closer to the concept of emptiness. Thus, the reflection phase is not necessarily restricted to the reasonings of the Madhyamaka. The integration of other thoughts can also be part of the "authentic imagination." Since we are dealing with the nature of reality and not a dogma based on belief, everything that contributes to a better understanding of duality and its dissolution – everything that pertains to authentic imagination – is beneficial, whatever the terms used or presentation formats.

The limits of intellectual understanding

The reasonings about emptiness are therefore considered as antidotes. But Rangjung Dorje makes it clear that these same reasonings can generate a perception that is even grosser than reality. How can an antidote also be a poison?

Intellectual understanding and liberation

It is possible in a first time to see the limits of intellectual understanding from the standpoint of liberation. The realization of emptiness must lead to the end of *saṃsāra,* it is considered as the remedy against suffering:

> On the other hand, examining phenomena, which have no self-entity, with discerning prajñā and meditating on that is the cause for attaining the result of nirvāṇa

No other cause pacifies suffering and mental afflictions completely. *Moonbeams*, p.216.

Additionally, emptiness is indissociable from limitless compassion[304]. How can the benefits that were previously presented contribute to that? It will be enough to take as example the case of afflictions to address this question. Let's remember that consciousness must purify the veils of affliction and the knowledgeable in order to be able to recognize its own nature. The first ones are grosser than the second ones – therefore, if it is established that the afflictions are not purified by intellectual understanding, it will be useless to look into the veils linked to dualistic grasping.

How are afflictions perceived through the understanding of emptiness that was previously described? Once the inexistence of objects in itself is demonstrated, do these objects stop absorbing consciousness? Personal experience is enough to realize that intellectually understanding the groundlessness of objects does not lead to recognizing their nature. Repeating this reasoning again and again will probably not lead to liberation. At best, this is another type of remedy to avoid getting carried away by afflictions, but this understanding cannot ignite a profound change in perception, neither generate the birth of infinite compassion[305].

It is not a direct perception

This finding cannot be explained by the nature of the intellect. Indeed, the latter is in conflict with its target. Reflection is essentially based on mental consciousness, while enlightenment is not conceivable in such framework. Understanding is the fruit of inferences, of reasonings – yet only direct perception perceives the absolute:

---

304 Wee section on awakened activity.

305 Guy Bugault has several inquiries on the consequences of the dialectic that pertains to emptiness: « L'agilité dialectique de Nāgārjuna nous a conduit [...] vers le constat d'une vacuité universelle. [...] Maintenant au moment de refermer ce livre, le lecteur se demandera peut-être ce qu'il lui reste de toute cette dialectique alors qu'il a surtout besoin de mettre son bon sens à l'épreuve de la vie quotidienne. Qu'en est-il donc de la vacuité au regard du bon sens ? » Bugault, 1994, p.325. He develops this inquiry in the pages that follow this citation (Bugault 1994, p.325-337). We will not present them here as he approaches the question through a different angle.

> It is only possible to realize the correct view by relying on the critical investigation of scriptures and reasonings because such critical investigation is conceptual analysis[306] that involves terms and referents, and Dharmakīrti has explained that that cannot determine [the view] as a direct cognition. *Moonbeams, p.88.*

We find this analysis again in the work of Zhönu Pal:

> This awareness cannot be grasped by the inferential valid cognitions of the Madhyamaka reasonings in the second *dharmacakra*, but must be realized directly. DRSM, 15.8-12[307].

Thanks to the reasonings, the groundlessness of "things" is understood, but this is a negation within the mental realm only. Yet, ignorance is not limited to an error of reasoning. For example, if we think that 2+2=5, a simple arithmetic reminder will lead us to correct this mistake. But illusion is not limited to this dimension. This is an ignorance that is metaphysical, which results from innate ignorance and imagined ignorance. It is profoundly rooted – it involves the body, senses, and a certain attitude towards existence that is rooted in the three poisons. As long as these factors are in place, reality cannot be perceived.

If the understanding of emptiness is not a direct perception, if it does not allow for an intimate perception of the world, it is then a new representation. By denying the self in such way, we are not dealing with true "emptiness" but with a new description of reality – "everything is empty," "all phenomena have no intrinsic existence." Consciousness therefore remains within references. We will see in the explanation of non-conceptual wisdom that the absolute cannot be based on a description. Otherwise, emptiness would become a new mental elaboration. Consciousness will then rebuild a world founded this time on an absence of self, and there will always be an "I" that extracts itself from experience. Zhönu Pal describes this phenomenon well in the following passage:

---

306 Tib. *sgra don can gyi rtog pa*. Litterally, « Sgra don can gyi rtog pa » does not correspond to "conceptual analysis" but to "a thought with a pronunciation and signification." The latter can be analytical or not (note from K.D. Mathes).

307 Mathes 2008, p.373.

> When meditating on this [negation], you search for another object, without thoroughly knowing yourself by yourself, and that is why dualistic appearances are not uprooted. Therefore mere [non-affirming negation] does not get one beyond the stage characterized by the mental imprints of ignorance. DRSM, 426.9-13[308].

Instead of eradicating all views, emptiness then becomes a new view.

Examples from Śāntideva and Candrakīrti

Jamgön Kongtrul Lodrö Thayé re-uses an example from *A Guide to the Bodhisattva's Way of Life* from Śāntideva, in order to illustrate that a knowledge – even valid from a superficial point of view – is not true from an absolute standpoint[309].

Let's imagine a dream in which we have a son, and the latter passes away. With the joy of his birth follows the pain of his death. When we realize that this son only existed in our dream, the sorrow of his disappearance fades away, since he did not actually exist. The reminder of his non-existence therefore allows us not the be affected. But is the thought "this child does not exist" nevertheless true? If we continue after the dream to say, "my son does not exist," this might be strange since we do not have a son. At one point, this thought is effective, but if we persist in keeping it alive, it misleads us. Therefore, it is not true in itself, but only in relation to what previously thought. It is the same thing with the understanding of emptiness. Thinking that everything is empty is useful to challenge the existence of the self of phenomena, but this is not about sticking with this thought all the time.

Nonetheless, we could object that unlike the example in which we punctually dreamed of being a mother or a father, we are constantly self-grasping. Shouldn't we then keep this idea of emptiness constantly in mind? Emptiness is the nature of phenomena, and it seems logical, therefore, to cultivate this idea. However, the point

308 Mathes, 2008, p.374.

309 NTC, Stanza 12.

here is on indicating that emptiness is not a new thought – there is a difference between thinking emptiness and realize or experience emptiness. If we stay at the level of emptiness by claiming that "everything is empty" or "nothing truly exists," we fall into an even grosser reality[310]. Jamgön Kongtrul Lodrö Thayé re-uses a citation from Saraha, in which he declares:

> Whoever clings to entities is like cattle,
> But whoever clings to the lack of entities is even more stupid.
> NTC Stanza 12 in *Luminous Heart* p.215.

Similar to the example of Śāntideva, the reasonings used here to put into question illusion are effective and true towards the initial situation. But if we remain at this stage, what appeared as liberating then becomes a poison. Someone constantly repeating to themselves that everything is emptiness is probably less problematic than someone constantly repeating that they do not have children. However, from a liberation standpoint, the individual is qualified as incurable:

> It is taught that emptiness is the remedy for reification, but if one fixates on
> emptiness, this is an incurable view.
> NTC Stanza 12 in *Luminous Heart* p.214.

In the case of assumption of emptiness as truly existing, Candrakīrti offers two examples to illustrate the absurdity of this hypothesis. The first one speaks of a man who, after a merchant told him "I have absolutely nothing to sell you," replies: "Ah! Give me this "absolutely nothing"!"[311]. The other example is that of a sick person who swallowed a drug to get rid of their mood disorder. If he perseveres in avoiding excreting the drug itself, this drug will make him even sicker[312]. If emptiness is taken as a view in

310 NT, Stanza 12.

311 *Prasannapadā Madhyamakavṛtti* (*Pr.*), 247, 5-6, passage extracted from Bugault 2002, p.173.

312 *Pr.* 248, 10 -249, 2, in Bugault 2002, p.173.

itself instead of as an instrument of liberation from views, no antidote is then possible against this belief, hence the incurability. Understanding emptiness would be then a theory defending the no-self, which - instead of uprooting ignorance - would lead the affected person into an even greater confusion. The functioning of consciousness remains the same with the sole change of replacing "existence" with "non-existence." Even if consciousness elaborates a reflection on the nature of the real based on the non-self, which is valid from a logical standpoint, this does not change anything on the existential realm. It is then knowledge that remains founded on mental elaborations[313], "everything is only emptiness" is then the equivalent of "all phenomena have a self."

When emptiness is grasped as object, two other attitudes are also possible. The first one entails suspending judgement. Since nothing can be founded on anything, then everything that appears is taken with perspective, without real engagement. The subject is not completely open to the world, it is still limited. Grasping onto emptiness can impact our current situation even more if it leads for example to a form of nihilism, a rejection of life or indifference.

The realization of emptiness necessitates another form of understanding

The intellectual understanding of emptiness does not fundamentally challenge our vision. The perceived object is less erroneous than before, but the relationship to the object, however, has not been modified[314]. To stop at the understanding of a lack of real existence

313 See DRSM, 6.15-18 in Mathes 2008, p.166.

314 Let's note that within the Dzogchen, the Prāsaṅgika-Madhyamaka is not considered as the highest vehicle, since it is only the third vehicle amidst a progression that contains nine of them. The Madhyamaka would be only a walk towards the Mantrayāna (Higgins 2012, p.110). It is also the idea of Rong-zom Chos kyi bzang-po, which expresses it several times in the *Introduction to the Way of the Great Vehicle* (*Theg-pa chen-po'i tshul la 'jug-pa*) : "The Madhyamaka, culminating point of the doctrine of the *Bodhisattvayāna*, would be incapable to surmount the opposition of two realities; going beyond these realities would be, according to this author, the characteristic of the *Vajrayāna*." Arguillère 2007, p.220). The problem of the Prāsaṅgika according to its authors is that the absolute is presented as an object of knowledge "without ever any worry about the essence or modalities of the knowledge that apprehends it""(Arguillère 2007, p. 296). David Higgins explains - based on the 18th chapter of the *Yid bzhin mdzod 'grel* from Longchenpa - that the two truths presented by the Prāsaṅgika pertain to the representational truth and not to

would be like reify emptiness and erase its true meaning:

> Nowadays it seems that most rely on their inferential rational cognition and take an abstract idea of emptiness as their mental object. The way that leads to an intellectually fabricated, partial emptiness (an analytical emptiness, an emptiness of the inanimate, and so forth) was discussed already with references to scriptures and reasonings. *Moonbeams*, p.219[315].

Approaching emptiness through sole logic does not allow a radically different way of being to arise. If we think emptiness without applying emptiness to its own thoughts, liberation is not possible. This endeavor remains an antidote until a certain point, yet we must then develop a direct perception of the nature of phenomena. The reasonings of the Madhyamaka set the stage for a direct access to consciousness but are not the end of the path. With logic, we negate a grasping of ordinary language, where we have to go beyond language itself, in the negation of negation and affirmation. In other words, subject and predicate must be put into question. What seems to only be a debate on logic has actually important consequences at an existential level.

The teachings of Buddhism are to be considered only as a raft and not as an end point[316]. Reflection allows for the development of a vision that we must also go beyond, so that it does not become a new straitjacket. Reflection is only a means to go back to what is primal, true knowledge lies outside of any frame, outside of any reference point. The absence of a self must be felt fully. Going beyond remedies is illustrated by the image of two pieces of woods that are rubbed against one another:

> When the imagination that is non authentic
> Meets the imagination that is authentic
> Imagination is freed up, just as two wooden sticks burn

principle-based knowledge (Higgins 2012, p.111).

315 See also *Moonbeams*, p.92.

316 Rahula, p.11.

> [when rubbed against one another].
> The grasping of the four characteristics
> What is to be abandoned, the remedies, suchness, and realization
> Is liberated. NT, Stanza 25 [122-126].

By dint of rubbing two pieces of wood against one another, fire arises and the two pieces of wood disappear. Similarly, by confronting non-authentic imagination and authentic imagination again and again, the fire of wisdom arises and makes all visions disappear, including that of emptiness. False conceptions and antidotes naturally free themselves, opening space for a direct perception. The two pieces of wood illustrate the grasping of what needs to be abandoned and the grasping of remedies, which arise on the path of accumulation and unification. At first, consciousness grasps onto false conceptions (what needs to be abandoned). This is why it applies remedies. In order for the remedies not to be, in turn, grasped onto, focus must be kept on suchness. When suchness is realized, consciousness sees emptiness directly. Then, the *bodhisattva* purifies their perception amidst the bhūmis until perfect non-grasping.

Third Turning and the no-self of phenomena : Buddha state, emptiness, emptiness-luminosity

The reasonings on emptiness are antidotes only if this intellectual understanding is pursued with means that do not only engage mental consciousness. It is necessary to eradicate all views, including those of emptiness itself in order to avoid a state of incurability:

> Kāśyapa, those who have views about the person that are as big as mount meru are better off than those who proudly entertain views about emptiness. Why is this? Kāśyapa, as emptiness means to emerge from all views, I declare that those who have views about this very emptiness are incurable. NTC Stanza 12[317], in Luminous Heart p. 214.

317 Quotation from *Ratnakūṭa* (*Sutra of the Heap of Jewels*).

Eradicating the view of emptiness is like bringing down the walls that trap the "I." At this stage of progression, consciousness is still inside of a configuration body-consciousness-thought, and that is what needs to be opened.

Realizing authentic emptiness renders the luminosity[318] of consciousness manifest, hence the association of the third turning with luminosity[319]. The term is often present in Buddhist literature[320], we especially find it in the *Supreme Continuum:*

> Illuminating, radiating, and purifying,
> and inseparable from each other, analytical wisdom,
> primordial wisdom, and total liberation
> correspond to the light, rays, and orb of the sun[321]. *Buddha Nature,* p.31.

The stake of this new part will be to determine what is the luminosity of consciousness[322]. After exposing a couple of meditation to go beyond any point of reference, we will try to understand the cognitive transformation associated with luminosity and why it implies bliss and a limitless awakened action.

Meditation techniques

The image of the two pieces of wood mentioned in stanza 25 is evocative, but it does not really give us the details of the process itself. It gives the impression that recalling again and again the fruits of reflection about absolute truth is enough to be able to dissolve duality. However, this way of doing has high chances to be kept at the level of mental consciousness. Other means therefore

318 Sct. *prabhāsvara*, tib. *'od gsal.*

319 See DRSM, 46.5-17, in Mathes 2008, p.245-246 and p.371.

320 Ruegg 1969, « La luminosité naturelle de la Pensée », p.409-454.

321 *Shes rab ye shes rnam grol rnams/ gsal dang 'phro dang dag phyir dang/ tha dad med phyir 'od dang zer/ nyi ma'i dkyil mkhor rnams dang mtshungs/* RGV, I.93/ 80.

322 The luminosity of consciousness is a concern of Buddhism since the pāli canon. See Ruegg 1969, pp. 412-437 ; Higgins 2012, p.79 ; 141.

seems necessary in order for perception to transform deeply and be free of mental elaborations. Thus, even if the image is well-chosen, more details are required to understand how to allow the fire of wisdom to arise.

The instructions allowing the development of a penetrating vision allow us to make the link between authentic imagination and direct vision of reality. Dakpo Tashi Namgyal explains that meditating on the nature of consciousness is necessary for emptiness not to be inert, not to limit itself to a simple intellectual understanding[323]. When an intellectual certitude is set, our understanding must recognize directly the no-self of phenomena:

> Those of us who do not understand the suchness of mind mistake thoughts and appearances (such as forms and sounds) – which manifest as the expressive power of mind – to exist objectively as things other than mind. And yet ultimately they are only our own mind. *Moonbeams*, p.238.

"The empty nature of the mind" and "[Everything is only] manifestations of the mind" – this is what needs to be recognized and cultivated.

Meditation on the no-self of phenomena can make one think at first glance that meditation focuses on the external world. Yet, this is always a work on the perception of consciousness. Meditating on the external object would only be an artificial meditation, consciousness cannot go outside of itself. It must work on its own representations to touch the real. Numerous instructions are given on this topic, but only the most central ones will be presented: the instructions in relation with emotions[324], the objects of the six sensorial conscisounesses[325], and the absence of birth[326]. The exercises on emotions and sensorial consciousnesses aim to see the dynamic expression of consciousness: thoughts and emotions must be rec-

323 Meditating on emptiness is like meditating on the nature of consciousness. See *Moonbeams*, p. 218-219.

324 *Moonbeams*, p.242-243.

325 *Moonbeams*, p.243-244.

326 *Moonbeams*, p.250.

ognized as "empty" manifestations of consciousness. The instructions on the absence of birth emphasize more the empty aspect of experience.

Dakpo Tashi Namgyal gives other more advanced instructions in his work, as understanding deepens. The ten bhūmis, the thirty-seven factors of awakening or even the four yogas of the Mahāmudrā give some instructions on the progression of realization of supreme emptiness.

Recognizing the nature of afflictions

> First : determining thoughts. Adopt the essential points for body and the gazes as explained above. For a short time, rest evenly in clarity and emptiness, free from identification, without being distracted for an instant. Within that state, a strong, clearly evident, coarse thought, such as angry thought, may arise or you should provoke one. As soon as it pops up, look directly at it. Examine and analyze that thought repeatedly and systematically as explained before : What is its color and shape ? What is its abode and support ? Is its essence something that can be identified or does it have a manifestation ?
>
> If thoughts do not arise, there are no objects to examine and analyze. Therefore, allow a little distraction. Think about the harm someone, such as an enemy, may have done to you, and give rise to angry thoughts. Examine them. [...] *Moonbeams*, p.242-243.

In the posture on seven gestures, it is necessary to first establish consciousness in the unity of emptiness and clarity – a state of non-grasping where the clarity of experience can reveal itself. Then, the exercise suggests to generate an emotion by reminding oneself for example of a memory that generates anger, sadness, or joy within. Once the emotion is present, the analytical method is identical to that which is used in the context of the individual no-self. If the emotion generated truly exists, it must then possess a shape, a color, a location, a support, etc. If none of this is found, then the emotion loses its substantiality, consciousness sees that it does not really exist.

Through reflection, we come to the conclusion that nothing is substantial. In the case of an emotion arising, this allows us to remember that it does not truly exist. But we have previously seen that it is not enough to free us from this thought. It is only a reminder or an indication that another mode of consciousness is possible in the moment that it arises. From a single consciousness, both *saṃsāra* or *nirvāṇa* can manifest. Thanks to analytical meditation, consciousness can learn to see differently the emotion that it generated in a protected environment, which is that of meditation. Instead of getting caught up in all the discourses around the given emotion, consciousness will, in contrary, learn to recognize its nature and not let itself get trapped. Once consciousness will be trained to use this new vision, emotions will be recognized as movements without difficulty.

Recognizing the nature of sensorial objects

The others series of instructions pertains to all apparences:

> Next : determining appearances. The exalted Dakpo [Gampopa] taught that all manifestations of mind – whatever thoughts and appearances involving percepts and perceivers arise – are all included with the category of appearances. Nevertheless, to make this easy to understand, in this context the term « appearances » is used fot what appears to the six modes of consciousness, that is, forms and the like, which are perceived objects. Those are what are to be analyzed and examined. Appearances – what arise when the five sense faculties (such as the eyes) connect with the five objects (such as forms), which consist of karma and latent tendencies – are known to ordinary people as direct [experiences]. *Moonbeams*, p.243.

Ordinary consciousness does not only solidify emotions, but also everything that appears to it. The process of perception described in the first part indicates that the first instant is without concept. Then, the following instant, mental consciousness names what sensorial consciousnesses received. The transfer between both happens almost automatically. The object is recognized according to some characteristics, it is identified immediately and designated by a very precise signification. Ordinary consciousness selects the information that it can recognize, that which have been identified in the past. The repetition of this process leads to an externalization of what is perceived. Additionally, the afflicted mind not only tends to want to grab onto the sensorial information that is received, but it also constraints the sensorial consciousnesses to operate in a restricted and dual way. It does not leave them the time to see in a different way, to deploy their own other faculties.

The exercise is an invitation to see that everything is a projection of consciousness. The nature of apparencies can be recognized by observing the six sensorial consciousnesses and their respective objects:

> Specifically, they are the inevitable shared appearances for the sense consciousnesses and seem to be objectively existent with their own features, such as color and shape. That being so, here we do not break down those appearances of external objects (such as forms) into particles, directions, and the like, and do not examine and analyze that they lack any nature. Since it is said that once we determine [the nature of] the perceiving mind, the fetters of perceived objects are self-liberated, now the object of analysis is primarily the mind that is the perceiver of appearances.
>
> As before, with your mind in a state of clarity-emptiness, cause an appearance of a form to arise vividly. When it does, carefully examine the mind perceiving that in terms of its color and shape, abode and support, identity and manifestation, as previously explained. Using the analysis of forms as the pattern, examine the perceiver of sounds, smells, and so forth. Similarly, examine and analyze the perceiver of whatever occurs or whatever you cause to occur : specific beings or things that are part of your environment, mental afflictions (such as attachment or agression), and any other kind of subtle or coarse manifestation, including happiness or sadness. *Moonbeams*, p.243-244.

Once again, the meditator allows a particular form to arise, a visual object to start, and it looks at whether this shape perceived by consciousness has a characteristic that allows them to claim that this object is "truly" this or that. This process must be applied to the other types of sensorial objects – sounds, odors, taste, feelings. The text also suggests at the end to take up again as object of meditation the afflictions or a particular experience. This excerpt clearly outlines that this reflection must not be led through reflection only: "We should not analyze them by decomposing them in minute directional parts. We must especially examine the consciousness that apprehends all appearances."

Arriving to the certainty that everything that arises is unborn

The previous exercises mainly aimed at realizing the nature of the diverse appearances, seeing that everything that arises is the dynamic expression of consciousness. Recognizing the nature of what is perceived allows for the dissolution of duality, because the perceiving subject and perceived object are not perceived as two distinct entities. By developing, in such way, the certainty that consciousness and appearances are inseparable, experience becomes much more flexible, and the subject realizes that they can have a direct action on what they are experiencing.

It is possible to deepen the recognition of consciousness's nature by realizing that it is unborn. Everything that has been accomplished before has already largely contributed to strongly cutting into duality, but another form of grasping can still be present, thus keeping consciousness amidst a certain configuration. Indeed, it is common to think that the different lived experiences of consciousness come from a specific place, from *a* consciousness – *a* consciousness where different personality traits and knowledges[327] would be stored. However, even if it is theoretically necessary to present a coherent model of the working of consciousness, in reality, consciousness is unborn, it does not intrinsically exist. The following instruction should allow the practitioner to see this directly. This practice is about eliminating any grasping of a "source consciousness":

327 In the end, this is what the presentation of the *ālayavijñāna* slightly suggests.

> Now look directly at what is simply labeled « mind », thinking, « What is its basic state, its abiding state, like ? »
>
> First, examine and analyze the causes from which mind arises. [...] In the middle, examine the way mind abides. [...] In the end, examine how mind departs. Since there is no place it goes or trail left behinf and no one able to end it or stop its manifestations, you conclude that it does not perish or terminate.
>
> Furthermore, if this mind-itself is something in the past, it has necessarily ceased or been destroyed. If it is something in the future, it has not yet arisen or emerged. If it is something in the present, it must be something that can be identified. Thus, since it cannot be analyzed as something present in one of the three times, it is free from the extreme of being existent. [...] Since it is free from arising, abiding, and ceasing, it is continuous. Since – realized or not – it is neither good nor bad, it does not fluctuate. It is present in all who do not recognize it, and thus it is neither attained nor lost. Always unchanging, it does not diminish. *Moonbeams*, p.250-251.

These instructions about the absence of birth can be divided in two parts. The examination of the primal cause, of prolongation of thoughts and their destination, pertains to meditating on space. Then the instructions pertain to a meditation on time.

How to apply these instructions?

While reading these instructions, a risk of "intellectualizing the practice" arises. Indeed, the guidance is given thanks to questions or indications on what needs to be realized, but the method of investigation is not clearly made explicit. For example, during meditation on afflictions, "we observe or deliberately make appear," "we look directly and we analyze it." Unlike the *Satipaṭṭhāna sutta*, we can notice that few indications are given to on how to observe or how to look directly. The term "analysis" can even mislay us away from the object of practice and lead us in the faults exposed in the second turning of the wheel.

In his *Treasury of Philosophical Tenets*[328], Longchenpa writes:

> The Mantra[yāna] brings about a direct recognition of the profound as follows. Without recourse to logical reasoning, one simply works directly with the vital points of body, speech, the energy channels, currents and potencies. In this way, one ascertains nonconceptual primordial knowing that is not a mental construct [but] the very quintessence of dharmakāya as the ground. Higgins 2012, p.243.

Thus, resorting to specific physical practices can be an alternative or a complement. Stanza 21 of the *Treatise on Pointing Out Buddha Nature* and its commentary confirm that a link between body and consciousness indeed exists:

> The mind appears as if it were a mind, and the mind [also] appears as if it were a body, thus existing as two aspects. From among these, the body is what [appears] subsequently, hence appearing from the aspect that [seems] to be a mind. *The Profound Inner Reality* says:
>
> Thus, the triad of nāḍī, vāyu, and tilaka
>
> appears from the aspect that is mind[329]. NTC, stanza 21, in *Luminous Heart* p.226.

Regarding the instructions on the sensorial objects and unborn consciousness, the following works from Tarthang Tulku offer interesting trails: *The Joy of Being*[330] et *Time, Space and Knowledge : A new vision of reality*[331].

---

328 Tib. *Grub mtha ' mdzod.*

329 We find this same idea in the Dzogchen : "In this connection, it is important to remember that open awareness abides both as the natural condition of mind (*sems nyid*) and as «embodied awareness» which makes its presence felt through the «vital centres of one's lived body» (*lus kyi gnad*) , particularily the heart, head, eyes and bioenergetic channels (rtsa)". Higgins 2012, p.85 and see also note 219 p.85.

330 Dharma Publishing, 2016 (revised edition).

331 Dharma Publishing, 1977.

Cognitive transformation

The 3rd Karmapa starts his explanation of Buddhahood from stanza 13, just after having mentioned the dangers of grasping onto emptiness[332]. A new terminology is deployed to characterize what manifests itself when emptiness is realized. Consciousness is designated by "natural consciousness," [333] "*dharmadhātu*"[334], "heart of the victorious ones," and Jamgön Kongtrul Lodrö Thayé adds "*dharmakāya*," "great bliss" and "*prajñāpāramitā*"[335]. The 3rd Karmapa then resorts to the different wisdoms – the wisdom similar to a mirror[336], the wisdom of equality[337], the discriminating wisdom[338], and the wisdom of all accomplishments[339].

"Wisdom" corresponds to the Tibetan term "*ye shes*." We find again "*shes*" as for ordinary consciousness, "*rnam shes*." "*Shes*" can be translated by "knowledge" or "consciousness." Now, consciousness is "ye" and not "*rnam*" anymore. In other words, it is not superficial anymore, it does not divide anymore, but it perceives phenomena in a primordial or principle-based way[340]. Before proposing a description of these different wisdoms, non-conceptual wisdom[341] will first be contemplated. Indeed, the key of

332 The three last points *vajra* of the *Unsurpassable Continuum* explains awakening in details, the qualities of awakening, and awakened action. The 3rd Karmapa uses again the main aspects of each of these points.

333 Tib. *tha mal.*

334 Tib. *chos kyi dbyings.*

335 NTC, Stanza 13.

336 Tib. *me long lta bu'i ye shes.*

337 Tib. *mnyam pa nyid kyi ye shes.*

338 Tib. *so sor rtog pa'i ye shes.*

339 Tib. *bya ba grub pa'i ye shes.* The 3rd Karmapa dévelops more extensively these four wisdoms in the *rnam shes ye shes 'byed pa'i bstan bcos* (*Treatise on the Distinction between Consciousness and Wisdom*).

340 Orna Almogi led research on the term *ye shes* and notably on the meaning of the prefix *ye* (*Rong-zom-pa's Discourses on Buddhology: A Study of Various Conceptions of Buddhahood in Indian Sources with Special Reference to the Controversy Surrounding the Existence of Gnosis (jñāna : ye shes) as Presented by the Eleventh-Century Tibetan Scholar Rong-zom Chos-kyi-bzang-po*. Tokyo : The International Institute for Buddhist Studies, 2009): "Whatever the original meaning of the component *ye* in the word *ye shes* may have been, it seems that the tradition takes it to be 'primordial'". Cited in Higgins 2012, p.96-97.

341 Sct. *Nirvikalpakajñāna*, Tib. *mi rtog pa'i ye shes*. Stéphane Arguillère prefers to translate this term by "non-fictioning, principle-based knowledge" ("connaissance principielle non fictionnante", Arguillère 2008, p.212-214), and Étienne Lamotte chose « intuitive knowl-

Mahāmudrā is the understanding of this term[342].

Non-conceptual wisdom

The *Distinction between dharma and dharmatā*[343] presents in paragraph 32 three characteristics that define the sphere of experience of non-conceptual wisdom[344] : non-dual and inexpressible, absence of appearance, and presence of appearances.

> 1. The defining characteristics here encountered, Should be known to consist of the following three aspects, Since one effect is repose in pure being, Which means that one actually settles in pure being, The non-dualistic and inexpressible[345].

edge » in *Mahāyānasaṁgraha (Mahāyāna Summary)* from Asaṅga (chapitre VIII).

342 Mathes, 2008 p.390. Non-conceptual wisdom also plays an important role in the *Unsurpassable Continuum* since it is also considered as the cause that purifies the veils of affliction and of the knowledgeable (*Sgrib pa gnyis dang bral ba yi/ rgyu ni ye shes gnyis yin te/ mi rtog pa dang de yi ni/ rjes thob de ni ye shes 'dod/* RGV II. 7/148). It is also compared to the perfect maturation of the royal child (*Mi rtog pa'i ye shes rnam par smin pa bzhin.* I.141/121). The 3rd Karmapa follows the same interpretation since he writes that "*dhātu*" and "non-conceptual wisdom" are equivalent in his commentary of the text *Distinction between dharma and dharmatā* (Brunnhölzl 2009, p.90). He also mentions this term in his commentary of *The Hymn of dharmadhātu,* Stance 2 (Brunnhölzl 2007, p.208). In the *Treatise Pointing Out Buddha Nature*, Jamgön Kongtrul Lodrö Thayé only refers to it three times in his commentary of stanza 25.

343 *Dharmadharmatāvibhāga* : This is an important text in the tradition of the Mahāmudrā which has been rediscovered at the same time as the *Supreme Continuum* (Mathes 2008, p.2). According to the *Instructions on the Ratnagotravibhāga, Theg chen rgyud bla'i gdams pa,* Maitrīpa would have discovered again the instructions only (Mathes 2012, p.205). The 3rd Karmapa has written a commentary on this text, and he uses it to define non-conceptual wisdom (Brunnhözl 2009, p.171 et s.).

344 Title of the section: "The characteristics of wisdom in terms of effects" – in other words "which experiences does wisdom open?" (tib. *Ye shes de yi byed las sam spyod yul gyi mtshan nyid ci lta bu yin pa la 'jug pa*). The Tibetan text and the translation in English are presented in *Maitreya's Distinguishing Phenomena and Pure being,* [sct. *dharmadharmatāvibhāga,* tib. *chos dang chos nyid rnam par byed pa],* with commentary by Mipham, Snow Lion Publications, 2004, pp.148-157.

345 Tib. *De la mtshan nyid jug pa ni/ rnam pa gsum gyis shes bya ste/ chos nyid gnas pa nyid las ni/ gnyis su med cing brjod med pa/ chos nyid rab tu gnas phyir ro/.*

The first characteristic is presented in a negative way – non-conceptual wisdom is non-dual[346] and inexpressible[347]. If it is inexpressible, then non-conceptual wisdom must not be understood literally. In paragraph 36 of this same text, the author mentions five states that are not non-conceptual wisdom: the absence of mental engagement, complete transcendence, total appeasement, essence of forms, and grasping of an argument[348]. Complete transcendence and total appeasement are not considered here, because these states pertain to realizations due to specific meditative practices.

First and foremost, it is clarified that non-conceptual wisdom does not mean a state of absence of mental engagement. In the commentary from Mipham, the absence of mental engagement points to the absence of confusion between nouns and referents. Non-conceptual wisdom cannot be this realization, otherwise the perception of children or the unconscious would be realizations of the absolute[349]. We could also think that the absence of mental engagement means a state of consciousness without thoughts, but this interpretation is not valid either. Indeed, the illusion is not caused by the thoughts – the grasping is problematic. In this case, awakening cannot be the absence of thoughts because that would not uproot ignorance. Another indication could be mentioned in order to show that the absence of thoughts is not synonymous of wisdom. In the process of perception, it appeared that the first instant is without concept[350]. Concepts appear only in the following instant. Yet, in both cases, instant with or without concepts, consciousness is defined as ordinary. Therefore, it is not only the denomination, conceptualization or the presence of thoughts that

346 Tib. *gnyis su med.*

347 Tib. *brjod med pa.*

348 *yid la mi byed yang dag 'das/ nye bar zhi dang ngo bo'i don/ mngon rtags 'dzin pa rnam pa lnga/*
For the translation of « *ngo bo nyid kyi don* », we have followed the Sanskrit (*rūpasvabhāva*) because it presents fewer issues and transmits the meaning well. The Sanskrit text is available in the *Mahāyānasaṁgraha* from Asaṅga translated by Etienne Lamotte (1973).

349 "A mere lack of the process of thought whereby the elaborations associated with worldly conventions are conceptualized by mixing names with their referents is not what is meant by "non conceptual", just as there is no such conceptuality in the mindstream of a newly born child or in that of a calf, and so on, without this being what is implied by "non conceptual" here", *Maitreya's Distinguishing Phenomena and Pure Being* 2004, p.167.

350 Tib. *rtog med.* See § on the individual no-self.

are sources of illusion, the senses are also a great factor of duality because they are themselves prehensive.

In addition, non-conceptual wisdom is not comparable to the "essence of forms," which is matter. Indeed, non-conceptual wisdom is knowledge, it is not a state without consciousness or inert.

Finally, non-conceptual wisdom is not the "grasping of an argument."[351] In the opposite case, non-conceptual wisdom would be the equivalent of the understanding described in the second turning of the wheel.

The second characteristic of this wisdom is the absence of appearances[352] :

> 2. And one effect relates to appearances' absence,
>
> Where duality, assumption and formulation, Faculties, objects, principles of awareness, And vessel-like world's appearances are absent;
>
> So these correspond to there being no observation, No description, no ground and no appearances, No principles of awareness, and no place,
>
> Which is how the sutras express the traits. Defining original nonconceptual wisdom. DDV, Suite du §32.[353]

Saraha gives a similar description:

> Look and look at the primordially pure nature of space,
>
> And seeing ceases, Saraha[354].

This poses the question of the link between ordinary beings and awakened beings, between superficial truth and absolute truth. Does this mean that a Buddha would not share the world with ordi-

---

351 Sct. *bhūtārthacitrīkāra*, tib. *mngon rtags 'dzin pa*. Étienne Lamotte transcribes it from sanskrit as "description of reality."

352 Tib. *snang ba med.*

353 *Snang ba med las gnyis dang ni/ ji ltar mngon par brjod pa dang/ dbang po yul dang rnam rig dang/ snod kyi 'jig rten snang med phyir/ des na 'dis ni brtag med pa/ bstan du med pa gnas med pa/ snang ba med cing rnam rig med/ gnas med pa zhes bya ba ste/ rnam par mi rtog ye shes kyi/ mtshan nyid mdo bzhin brjod pa yin/*

354 Cited in *Moonbeams*, p.236.

nary beings? What then would perceive non-conceptual wisdom?

The third characteristic sheds light on this question, since non-conceptual wisdom is also defined by the presence of appearances:

> 3. And one effect relates to appearances's presence,
> Since experience of every phenomenon,
> Is equivalent to the center of open space,
> And formations all are appearances like illusions. DDV, Fin §32[355].

There is nothing to see, but at the same time a presence manifests itself[356]. A presence where all phenomena are compared to the center of the space, and the mental formations to illusions. These two characteristics can be associated to the wisdom of suchness and to the wisdom of diversity (or wisdom of multiplicity) respectively[357]. Indeed, in his commentary of *the Treatise on the Distinction between Consciousness and Wisdom*, Jamgön Kongtrul Lodrö Thayé writes that the wisdom similar to a mirror is the wisdom that knows

355 tib. *Snang ba las ni chos thams cad/ nam mkha' dkyil mnyam snang phyir ro/ 'du byed thams cad sgyu ma sogs/ lta bur snang ba yin phyir ro/.*

356 In the *Treatise on Pointing Out Buddha Nature*, the author uses two verbs to express the view: "lta" for the ordinary view and « mthong » for awakened vision (NT, stanza 19). At the ordinary level, consciousness is completely trapped in the illusion of the self. Then comes a phase of negation of the self (eradication of all views), which allows one to manifest the authentic *view.* "The difference is in the presence or not of dualistic grasping. If this was not the case, how could the activity of the victorious ones be in relationship [with the world]?" Stanza 30 [152-154].

357 The 3rd Karmapa uses these two types of wisdom in his commentary of stanza 5 in the *Hymn to the dharmadhātu* (Brunnhölzl 2007, p.219). Besides, Stéphane Arguillère defines omniscience based on these two types of wisdom:
"It is a constant thesis in the dogma of the Mahāyāna, the dogma according to which the Awakened one perceives all things, both in their absolute nature and in the detail of their superficial aspects. The science of the absolute is called "science of things as they are," and the science of surface is called "science of things as much as they are." The question of omniscience, which is to say, deep down, of the way that a Buddha perceives the world, is philosophically primordial: indeed, this vision is, by hypothesis, the ultimate right knowledge, the only perception perfectly adequate to the real. Of course, we can anticipate it in a very imperfect way only; nevertheless, the speculation on this question is not less fertile in many ways. To us, it is, with the concepts of primordial knowledge (tib. *ye-shes*) and Real Element (skt. *dharmadhātu*), the most fundamental issue of Buddhist philosophy." Arguillère 2002, p.81-82.

things as they are,[358] and the wisdom of equality, discriminating and all accomplishing are wisdoms that know phenomena in their diversity,[359] and perceive them as similar to an illusion[360].

The wisdom similar to the mirror or wisdom of suchness

Characteristics

The 3rd Karmapa uses the definition of wisdom similar to the mirror offered in the *The Ornament of the Mahāyāna Sūtras* :

> All wisdoms appear [in it] without any "mine."
> It is unconfined and ever present.
> It realizes all knowable objects, yet is never directed toward them[361].NY [112-114], in *Luminous Heart* p.292-293

In order to have an idea on the lived experience related to the mirrorlike wisdom, our explanation will be based on these couple of elements, as well as the meditative techniques previously presented[362].

---

358 Tib. *ji lta ba mkhyen pa'i ye shes.*

359 Tib. *ji snyed pa mkhyen pa.*

360 « These wisdoms can be summarized in the two categories of knowing suchness and knowing variety. as for the first, the nature of all phenomena—the ultimate lack of appearance—refers to the wisdom of knowing suchness in meditative equipoise. [...] The wisdom of knowing variety during subsequent attainment is the direct realization that all possible types of substances of all phenomena within the three times are illusionlike ». NYC, in *Luminous Heart,* p.29. tib. *Ye shes de dag kyang bsdu na ji lta mkhyen pa dang ji snyed mkhyen pa gnyis su 'du ste/ Dang po ni/ chos thams cad kyi chos nyid snang med mthar thug pa ni mnyam bzhag ji lta ba mkhyen pa'i ye shes yin te/ [...] Dus gsum kyis bsdus pa'i chos thams cas kyi rjas rigs ma lus pa thams cad sgyu ma lta bur mngon sum du rtogs pa ni/ rjes thob ji snyed pa mkhyen pa'i ye shes yin te/ [...]* Texte extrait du *rnam par shes pa dang ye shes 'byed pa'i bstan bcos kyi tshig don go gsal du 'grel pa rang byung dgongs pa'i rgyan*, [Jamgön Kongtrul Lodrö Tayé's commentary on NY], dans *mdo sngags mtshams sbyor*, vol. 1 Pages 357 – 412.

361 *Ye shes kun snang nga yir med/ yongs su ma chad rtag tu ldan/ shes bya rtogs shing der phyogs min/*
He uses the definition given in the le *Mahāyānasūtrālaṃkāra*, IX 68-69a.

362 The commentary from Jamgön Kongtrul Lodrö Thayé does not really help us here for a phenomenological analysis: « In that mirrorlike wisdom, all other wisdoms and all knowable objects appear, but without being grasped as "mine." Since it is unconfined, [mirrorlike wisdom] is ever present. Since it is free from all obscurations and not ignorant about

All wisdoms appear [in it] without any "mine"

In the part about ordinary consciousness, the "I" has been approached from the standpoint of the body and the consciousness. How to understand now the absence of "I" in these two realms?

The relationship to the body is again modified when Buddhahood is attained. Indeed, the meditation on the body offered in the *Satipaṭṭhāna sutta* is limited to the physical body in its grossest aspects. Attention lands on movements, anatomy, aging, death, or even sensations. But according to Rangjung Dorje – and from the standpoint of tantras more generally – it is possible to deepen bodily perception. Indeed, the body is also composed of *nāḍīs*, *vāyus* and *tilakas*[363], it is the energetic body or subtle body. The body is not only matter, it is, in reality, body-space. Thanks to the last practices, consciousness and physical body are less in duality; however, the realization of the subtle body is not yet established[364]. Experiences at this level can finally manifest, but no specific instruction is presented. The practices offered[365] to deepen the bodily perception allow for the realization that the body, in reality, has no substance "in itself."

---

the entirety of knowable objects, it is not directed toward the consciousnesses that are triggered by objects [107] and is free from not knowing. Hence, it realizes all knowable objects, yet is never apprehending them through being directed outward toward them», NYC [112-114], Brunnhölzl 2009, p.293. Otherwise, the theme of the mirror has been studied by Paul Demiéville in *Le miroir spirituel*. He evokes the mirrorlike knowledge as so: "We still find in this school [the epistemological school] an intriguing doctrine, the one of the four modes of transcendental knowledge which are specific to Buddhas and whose first knowledge's name is "mirrorlike wisdom." It is one aspect of omniscience. "Mirrorlike wisdom" consists in the following: all that can be known is perpetually reflected in the mind of Buddhas, without limitation of space and time, without possible error, and without the Buddhas ever being able to forget anything, but also without this knowledge being present to the Buddhas through a perceptive process and without affecting the Buddhas' own eternally pure nature. It is in this mirror that all living beings watch the objects of knowledge arise like reflections, in particular the objects of good and salvaging nature." Démiéville 1973, p.145-146 (our translation).

363 The details on this subtle body are found in the *Profound Inner Reality.* See also NTC, Stanza 21.

364 Experiences in relation to this more subtle level can also manifest themselves, but the practices of the *sutta* do not include this dimension.

365 These practices will not be described because they go beyond the framework of study that we chose. To find an approach, see for example Herbert Guenther, *The life and teachings of Naropa, Translated from Tibetan with Philosopical Commentary based on the Oral Transmissions.* Oxford: Clerendon Press. Reprinted: Shambala South Asia Editions, 1963.

> At this one moment, the flowers of marks bloom
> Within those who are endowed with a space-body. NT, Stanza 26, [127-128]

Thenceforth, the body is not an element that is well-delimited in space anymore. The limit between internal and external drawn by its contours is recognized as being only the product of thoughts and completely dissolved. What is more, the density of the body or even its opacity is not topical anymore. The experience of the body is space, but also clarity since its constitution manifests itself. The body is not a "me" as previously defined anymore – independent, indivisible and unique. This change in perception at the level of the body is a first consequence of the absence of mental elaborations – the body is perceived at first as a material entity, then as an impermanent phenomenon that can be separated into different elements, now the body is space without internal/external distinction. With the realization of the subtle body, the body is beyond the notion of pure and impure – it inspires no more fascination or defiance.

Just like the body, the nature of consciousness is often compared to space[366]. Specific mediation instructions are used to recognize this. By searching for the source, the duration, and the destination of thoughts, the practitioner is invited to see that consciousness is unborn. By understanding this directly, consciousness can stay in a state of openness. The thoughts (cognitive veils) and emotions (veils of afflictions) are not obstacles to overcome anymore. Because their nature is recognized, everything becomes more malleable. Thus, consciousness does not live in a space limited by different thoughts, references, or fixations, but remains in an open space with way more possibilities.

Mirrorlike wisdom refers also to the *dharmakāya* – the body of qualities. Let's remember that the realization of the subtle body implies an integration body-consciosuness, thus leading consciousness to a change in state where the consciousness-body duality does not exist anymore – the body is perceived as an aspect of conscious-

366 Moonbeams, p.236, see also the discussions on space in the third part.

ness, consciousness becomes part of the body. The *dharmakāya* manifests[367] without discontinuity in its numerous qualities, such as the ten strengths, the four wisdoms of self-confidence, or even the eighteen special attributes[368]. In other words, the re-discovering of space is not an empty space with nothing in it. Ordinary consciousness' space was filled with thoughts, judgments, emotions, and all of it held together very tightly while occulting everything upstream. But when all these elements are not grasped onto anymore, space dilates, what happens within that space becomes more fluid and other faculties can reveal themselves. In contrary to ordinary consciousness where space is perceived as a vessel containing things separated by nothing, awakened consciousness does not see "nothing" as pure absence. Nothing is not nothing. This empty space is also rich with qualities, it is dynamic. These qualities increase the clarity of consciousness as well as its action power.

> Let's examine again our example of the mirror: it is empty, which is to say without any inherent image; but its way of being empty is not that of a white wall without any ornament. It is an emptiness that is more radical, because if the white wall, at least, has its own color, the mirror doesn't. At the same time, this emptiness does not go without some sort of illimited fecundity, which is the limpidity specific to the mirror. Yet, this limpidity which is mainly due to the emptiness of the mirror illustrate what we call "la nature du Fond," which is said to be established spontaneously (lhun-grub), clear (gsal-ba), and infinite (ma-'gags). Arguillère 2007, p.385 (our translation).

The knowledge of the Buddhas is therefore is at one with the absolute. However, even if a cosmic and encompassing *dharmakāya*[369]is mentioned in certain places, the *Treatise On Pointing Out Buddha Nature* shows that this is not about an extinction of the continuum of consciousness. Only grasping is put into question. Let us

367 Sct. *lalita*, tib. *rol pa*.

368 NT, Stanzas 15-17.

369 Tib. *khyab pa* ; RGV, II 29/159 et II. 35/165.

remember that the critic of the self pertains to the afflicted mental only, and that the other face of the mental is the immediate mental. In other words, once the afflicted mental is purified, the continuity guaranteed by the immediate mental is always present but without the distortion. What is pure fiction is only the person built by the afflicted mental. Regarding the term "encompassing" or "omnipresent," it points first and foremost to omniscience[370]. Buddhahood is omnipresent because it knows the suchness of all phenomena. Therefore, non-duality implies the "no two" but also "no one." Denying duality is not about claiming a unity where a subject and object would become only one, in the literal sense of the term. This interpretation is only another extreme of dualistic thought. In other words, the self does not melt in a big Whole. "As such, the unity of *Buddhas* in the *Dharmakāya* does not exclude the preservation of their ipseity, although on a mode that is not familiar to common thought[371]."

Even if the description of ordinary consciousness can be applied to the whole of non-awakened beings, this does not imply that their lives are identical. The "content" or the life stories are completely different. It is the same for awakening. The cognition of a Buddha is described thanks to the wisdoms and *kāyas*, but each Buddha will have a different activity depending on their respective wishes and their link with beings[372].

It is unconfined and ever present.

The commentary of this verse is quite quick since it speaks for itself. Mirrorlike wisdom is always permanent and presents no interruption.

It realizes all knowable objects.

"Realizes" is the translation of the Tibetan verb "rtogs pa." It can also be translated by "understand directly" :

---

370 Cf. RGV II. 35/165 : "[Buddhahood] is omnicient because it knows all things."

371 Arguillère 2007, p. 442 (our translation).

372 « The reason for this happening lies in the coming together of three [factors]— the blessing influence of the victors, the power of their [former] aspiration prayers, and the pure karma of those to be guided », NTC Stanza 31, in *Luminous Heart* p.240.

> One must know that *rtogs pa* most often designates an adequate, immediate understanding without concept, born from a meditative practice and not only a study. Arguillère 2008, p.211.

The understanding of the knowledgeable is not a knowledge based on representations, but a direct perception. The question left to inquire about is how the wisdom of suchness can know *all* of the knowledgeable. What does it perceive directly?

A first element of response can be given in stanza 2 in the Treatise *On Pointing Out Buddha Nature:–*

> The *dhātu* of time without beginning
> Is the site of all the *dharmas*. NT, Stanza 2 [5-6].

The *dhātu* is one of the terms that are used to designate the nature of consciousness. It is used to emphasize its causal aspect[373]. Indeed, by being the place of all phenomena, the *dhātu* is comparable to their fundamental cause – *dhātu* is the site where everything deploys itself. Rangjung Dorje has the care to write "the *dhātu* of time without beginning" and not only "the *dhātu*." We can hypothesize that the expression "*dhātu* of time without beginning" insists on the idea that the *dhātu* permeates everything, by establishing a strong relationship between the *dhātu* and phenomena. Indeed, the time and phenomena are indissociable since expresses itself through phenomena. What is more, qualifying time as "without beginning" is like denying temporality as it is perceived by ordinary consciousness, and thus leaves room manifestation in its whole integrality. Consequently, associating the *dhātu* and time without beginning is like making manifestation and *dhātu* identical. Thus, the *dhātu* is not only a space where phenomena appear, a place where events happen like theaters do for theatrical pieces, but it is also their heart, *dhātu* permeates everything. As such, the *dhātu* is comparable to a matrix. By precising that the *dhātu* is not only the place of all phenomena but that the *dhātu* of time without beginning is the place of all phenomena, the *dhātu* cannot be considered

373 cf. NT et NTC, Stance 5.

only as an inert space where different scenarios of existence would unfold. *Dhātu* and phenomena are of the same nature: the *dhātu* is a dynamic space and not a passive space.

A last point to go over before responding to our initial question. What phenomena is he talking about? *"Chos"* in Tibetan can both designate internal and/or external phenomena. What is its meaning here? Jamgön Kongtrul Lodrö Thayé writes that the *dhātu* is also named "*ālaya*" or "base of everything[374]":

> The basic element [*dhātu*] of time without any previous beginning [...] is the matrix or support of all afflicted and purified phenomena. Therefore, as a general name, it is called "ālaya." NTC, Stanza 2, in *Luminous Heart* p. 206.

> The ālaya, from which all seeds rise,
> Is held to be the nature of [everything] internal and external[375]. NYC [62-63] in *Luminous Heart* p. 277.

The *ālaya* is named "all-ground consciousness" first because of this function as "reservoir" or "receptacle" that it fulfills by conserving the different tendencies sowed by our actions; but the *ālaya* is also the cause of phenomena's manifestation. In other words, our tendencies will not only color what we perceive, but they are also the origin of the environment in which we live. Thus, the given phenomena are both internal and external.

"The whole of the knowledgeable" pertains to all phenomena, and awakened consciousness can know it directly thanks to the identity of nature between the *dhātu* and phenomena. This element

---

374 Jamgön Kongtrul Lodrö Thayé uses the term « kun gzhi » (sct. *ālaya*) to designate the *dhātu*. Yet, in stanza 6 of the root text, the 3rd Karmapa uses this term to designate impure consciousness. Additionally, in the presentation of the eighth consciousness in the *Treatise on the Distinction between Consciousness and Wisdom*, which also comes under ordinary thus impure consciousness, the 3rd Karmapa uses « *kun gzhi rnam shes* » (sct. *ālayavijñāna*). This floating in the terminology reflects a controversy that comes back to at least the arrival of Buddhism to Tibet. David Higgins retraces the evolution of these terminological terms, see Higgins 2012, p.136-178; also see Schaeffer 1995, note 17 p.95; Frauwallner 1951, p.148 ; Ruegg 1973, p.35 ; Mathes 2008, p.48 et 61.

375 *Vajraśikhara[mahāguhya]yogatantra* (tib. *Sa bon kun ldang kun gzhi ni/ phyi dang nang gi bdag nyid 'dod/*).

contributes probably to the definition of omniscience[376] of a Buddha.

... yet is never directed toward them

"*Phyogs*" translated by "directed toward" implies the idea of a direction. We can hypothesize that this term can be applied here to the mastery that conscience has on what it perceives.

Ordinary consciousness is absorbed by the perceived object, maintaining it outside of its own self – it is attracted to the outside. Consciousness tends to identify with its thoughts and to get carried away by emotions without taking a step back. As for the *arhat* themselves, they do develop a certain distance.

When a mental event arises or when an object is perceived, the *arhat* will know how to avoid getting carried away. However, as we emphasized before, the arhat does not recognize the nature of that which appears. They elaborate or fabricate a strategy to face what arises, for example by reminding themselves that "everything is impure" or that "everything is impermanent." Therefore, the *arhat* is still ruled or directed by something that remains fabricated. As of the perception of a Buddha, it is not ruled by the knowledgeable. Since the main difference between an arhat and a Buddha is the recognition of the nature of consciousness and all phenomena, we can suppose that it is this knowledge that makes the consciousness of a Buddha unaffected by any circumstance. A Buddha's consciousness recognizes the nature of what arises, it realizes that there is no difference in nature between what is perceived and the one who perceives. Everything is the play of manifestation. Thanks to this, it is possible to create a relationship with any type of object without becoming absorbed or ruled. Like space, consciousness is never affected by what arises. The example of the mirror can illustrate this:

> Given a mirror: whichever image appears in it, the mirror stays, so to speak, always clean, without any disturbance, immaculate in itself, innocent, as if it had never reflected anything. The mirror has a particular way to be empty: as varied as the reflections which appear on it can be,

376 Tib. *thams cad mkhyen pa.*

> these are not the mirror, they do not interest its being, which stays true to its self, both indeterminate (without a fixed shape or color) and perfectly determined (always conserving itself as it is, on its own terms). Arguillère 2007, p.384.

Center of space

The wisdom of a *buddha* is said to be similar to a mirror, not only because it perceives phenomena as they are, but it also because it recognizes its face in everything, without being affected. "I" is not at the center anymore, and everything is comparable to space. Therefore, in a certain way, every phenomenon is at the center. Everything is perceived in interrelation at the most subtle level and in its totality, in the three times and in all directions

Wisdom of multiplicity

The other wisdoms characterize more specifically the way of knowing appearances – they know phenomena in their diversity, and they "appear [in mirrorlike wisdom][377].

Wisdom of equality - one flavor only

> [When] the three veils purify themselves, the mental resting [on the foundation of everything]
>
> [Becomes wisdom] of everything, [supreme] peace. NT, Stanza 36 [173-174].
>
> There are no afflictions, no existence[378], and no peace[379]. NY [120] in *Luminous Heart*, p.295.

When the veils of afflictions, of the knowledgeable, and of meditation are purified, the afflicted mental becomes wisdom of equality.

377 NY [112].

378 *saṃsāra*.

379 *Nyon mongs med cing srid zhi med/*

This realization results in the absence of afflictions and supreme peace.

The term "supreme" associated to "peace" signifies that consciousness is free of all forms of duality. At this stage, consciousness recognizes that everything is of the same nature, it realizes the even and homogeneous flavor of phenomena. The notions of "pure" or "impure," "good" or "bad" are not references of consciousness anymore. As opposed to the *arhat* who is in a fabricated peace, at a distance from the saṃsāra, the realization of the even and homogeneous flavor allows consciousness to not be in a "fabricated calmness" anymore. Consciousness can access tranquillity in a more dynamic way by recognizing that "everything is perfect," "everything is pure," nothing is good or bad in itself. The different values attributed to events are only mental elaborations. There is therefore "no affliction, no saṃsāra, no peace." This does not imply being "above morality" or "above ethics," but the relationship to what arises is different.

Discriminating wisdom

> The mental formations [of a *Buddha*] appear [as] birthing and disappearing momentarily
> Similar to impure mental formations.
> If it was not that way,
> The activity of the *rūpakāyas* would be interrupted.
> Yet, we do not express it through the name of "mental formation,"
> But by "discriminating wisdom." NT, Stanza 28 [142-147].

The beginning of this stanza indicates that Buddhas have mental formations. Can it be concluded that the thoughts of a Buddha are no different than that of an ordinary being? In no case, since this is about discriminatory wisdom[380]. Thus, a clear distinction is made between ordinary thoughts and awakened thoughts. What is this difference?

380 Tib. *so sor rtog pa'i ye shes*.

Discriminatory wisdom is the result of a change in state of the mental (sixth consciousness) and in the mental that is immediate. In the *Treatise on the Distinction between Consciousness and Wisdom*, Jamgön Kongtrul Lodrö Thayé describes this wisdom as "the wisdom that knows all phenomena without hindrance, in their diversity and in distinct ways, in the instant[381] and without confusion'[382].

"Without hindrance" probably refers to the way of knowing that is direct. No mental representation shields what is perceived. This way of knowing allows a perception that is much richer, unlike indirect perception, which impoverishes reality. Additionally, this wisdom is able to know the multitude of phenomena with more precision, in a more distinct way. Finally, we have translated "*ma 'dras*" by "without confusion". "'*dra*" generally means "similar," we use it to compare two things that are similar. There is also the verb "'*dra ba,*" which means "to cut." Since ordinary consciousness considers its representations as absolute truth – or we could say that it considers them as similar to absolute truth – and through this bias, consciousness cuts its self away from reality, "*ma 'dras*" could mean the inverse effect – once ignorance dissipates, this confusion does not happen anymore.

Thus, the mental formations of awakened beings are not similar to that of non-awakened beings. Even if a *bodhisattva* or a *buddha* have thoughts as ordinary beings do, which appear and disappear over time, there is a difference, and that is why we talk about discriminatory wisdom and not mental formations anymore.

Discriminatory wisdom also possesses qualities that provide it with knowledge of non-physical worlds. These are qualities that are linked to the *sambhogakāya*. The commentary indicates for example that the *buddhas* perceive all worlds night and day, and they know simultaneously the different streams of being.

All accomplishing wisdom

Through this, the five sense faculties change state,

381 This aspect will be discussed at a later stage.

382 Our translation, *Shes bya ji snyed pa de snyed so sor skad cig gis ma 'dras par thogs pa med par mkhyen pa'I ye shes te/* (Brunnhölzl 2009, p.297: « It is the wisdom of unimpededly knowing all phenomena in their entirety in a distinct, instantaneous, and unmixed way »).

> Mastering engagement in all objects[383]. NY [147-148], in *Luminous Heart*, p.301.

> The nature of the great elements etc., is grasped [by ordinary beings]
> And reveal their powerful essence.
> Whether it is [from the standpoint] of illusion or absence of illusion,
> There is absolutely no difference at the level of appearance. NT, Stanza 29 [148-151].

The sensorial faculties of the five senses and of mental consciousness become all-accomplishing wisdom. Before, the five senses and mental consciousness were dominated by dualistic grasping. The sensorial objects perceived seemed of a different nature than that of consciousness, and therefore seemed external. With all accomplishing wisdom, the senses can deploy their faculties, like the possibility to act directly on elements. Whether from the ordinary or awakened standpoint, appearances do not change. A Buddha and an ordinary being will perceive, if they are in nature for example, the same landscape. But the wisdom of a Buddha has power on the elements – earth, water, air, fire – which ordinary consciousness does not have, because appearances are perceived as external to consciousness, and they are apprehended through specific names and characteristics. At the awaken level, matter and the notion of frontier is a recognized as mental elaborations. Jamgön Kongtrul Lodrö Thayé takes the example of a magician to illustrate this difference. When the magician manifests their illusion, they see the same thing as their spectators. However, they do not grasp onto this illusion as if it existed independently to them, and they can also act on it knowing what they are constituted of[384]. This

383 *Dbang po lnga rnams gnas gyur ni/ don kun 'jug /*

384 See NTC stanza 30. A passage of the *Unsurpassable Continuum* also indicates that the six consciousnesses have a relationship to the world that is different at the stage of awakening, these are the six pure sensorial faculties (RGV, II.18/154). The stanzas II.19-20/155 of the *Unsurpassable Continuum* give a couple elements that describe the experience of the six consciousnesses: « [This essence is the cause that permits], Seeing the forms not [constituted] by the [four] elements, Hearing the good and pure words, Smelling the pure

stanza clearly indicates that awakened perception always apprehends object, but on a different mode. "Consequently, even if the appearances of those who are being guided appear to the *Buddhas'* wisdom of diversity, the latter does not conceptualize them, just as the mirror is free from grasping and concepts when images appear in it" [385].

All accomplishing wisdom is associated to the *nirmāṇakāya*. A Buddha can take whichever body to accomplish the benefit of others.

Phenomena are comparable to an illusion.

Let's come back to paragraph 32 of the *Distinction between Dharma and Dharmatā*, where it is specified that "all mental formations are appearances comparable to illusions" [386]. The term "illusion" can seem pejorative. Indeed, it points more to ideas of cheating, falsehood, error...than to any form of wisdom. Yet, when the 3rd Karmapa shows the essence of Buddhas' heart, he writes:

> All [phenomena] are neither true nor delusive.
> Scholars claim that they are comparable to the [reflection of] the moon on water. NT, Stanza 13 [48-49] [387].

This example of the moon on water is used by the Madhyamaka to illustrate superficial truth. As of the absolute truth perceived by

[perfume] of the ethics of *sugatas*, Tasting the savor of the noble excellent *dharma* of the Mahā[yāna], Experimenting the bliss of the *samādhi*, Knowing its deep teaching by nature (*'byung med gzugs don blta dang gtam bzang ni/ btsang ma mnyan dang bde gshegs tshul khrims kyi/ dri gtsang smon dang 'phags chen dam chos ro/ myong dang ting 'dzin reg bde nyams myong dang/ rang gi ngo bo nyid kyi zab pa'i tshul/ rtogs pa'i rgyur gyur zhib mor bsams pa na/*).

385 NTC, Stanza 33.

386 In the NTC, Jamgön Kongtrul Lodrö Thayé also uses the term of "simple appearance" (tib. *tsam snang*; Stanza 13, or « mere appearance » Brunnhölzl 2009, p.216).

387 Stanza 13 of the *Treatise on Pointing Out Buddha Nature* uses the *Yuktiṣaṣṭikā* (*Sixty Stanzas of Reasoning* - Brunnhölzl 2009, note 531 p.453) by comparing all phenomena to the reflection of the moon on the water. For the other references to the two truths in the work of the 3rd Karmapa, see Brunnhölzl 2009, p.87-89.

awakened beings, it is characterized by non-dualistic wisdom[388]. In this tradition, the two truths are neither distinct nor identical while still being inseparable[389].

In his commentary on the *Madhyamakālaṅkāra*, Mipham describes this inseparability in the following way:

> What we call the "superficial" should be, from the standpoint of childish beings, only understood as a certain something, like the production, which by its manifestation, would occult emptiness and obscure it. But [in truth], it must not be understood as completely misleading and untruthful; one must not believe that it always hides emptiness. Indeed, for the Ārya, void and conditioned production illustrate themselves reciprocally. Arguillère 2007, p.290.

Wanting to associate deception to the superficial is like falling back to the superficial. Phenomena are not real because they are not established substantially, but they do not deceive either since the different appearances manifest themselves, and they "contain" within themselves the absolute. Superficial truth is not unreal or set aside, it is simply perceived with more depth, and it is much more malleable, flexible. As grasping dissolves over time, what was considered substantial loses of its strength. This, however, does not become non-being, or something unreal that one should get rid of[390]. If the illusion must be understood as a mistake, then it points

388 Let's note that in this context, only the reflection is taken into account to illustrate the inseparability of the non-self and appearances, the moon that causes the reflection is not taken into account. This exclusion limits the impact of the example, since the objective is to show the possibility of an appearance despite the absence of a self, but in the example, the reflection is indeed the reflection of something.

389 This formulation of the two truths prevent unfortunate consequences described in the *Unveiling of the Profound Meaning Sūtra* (See Lamotte 1935, chapter 3).

390 This interpretation of the two truths by the 3rd Karmapa makes him stand out from Dolpopa and Tsongkhapa. For a detailed explanation, see Arguillère 2007 (pp. 231-246 and pp.288 and following, 2008. With Dolpopa, "all of reality falls on one side of the absolute, and in a way, all of duality one the sole side of the superficial, thus, the unreal. Having said that, a true integration of the two realities, absolutes and superficial, is lacking" (Arguillère 2007, p.216). Additionally, « la connaissance principielle substrat universel (*kun-gzhi ye-shes* / *ālayajñāna), absolute reality, is of course the *base* or the *foundation* (*rten, gzhi*) of consciousness (*rnam-shes, vijñāna*), superficial reality, but it is not its cause" (Arguillère 2007,

to substantiality.

This inseparability of the superficial and the absolute is the meaning of "the form is emptiness, the emptiness is the form." The phenomenon lacks any existence of its own, that's precisely why it can manifest itself:

> In the *Madhyamaka,* I find absolutely nothing, in spite of the undeniable apparent presence of the examined thing. According to a traditional example, it is like the reflection of the moon on the water, which shines clearly and is drawn distinctly in front of our eyes, but disperses as soon as one tries to grasp it, to the re-form soon after: an existence purely phenomenal, which does not *resist* to the critical examination yet *insists* in the thoughtless and spontaneous perception, Arguillère 2002, p.60.

The ordinary view is stuck on the superficial, trapped in laws that are only constructions of consciousness. The awakened view, however, without denying the superficial, perceives a vaster, deeper dimension. We are not any more in the presence of a partial consciousness but of a consciousness or wisdom of diversity which perceive the principle of phenomena. This is the wisdom of suchness[391].

---

p.214 and Stearns 1999, p.217 note 14). Finally, another point – ordinary consciousness seems to be considered as filth in Dolpopa through the example of clouds obstructing the sky. These three points are sufficient to show that the 3rd Karmapa does not share the same interpretation as Dolpopa's (Arguillère 2007, p.215. For a more comprehensive list of the differences between the 3rd Karmapa and Dolpopa, see. Brunnhölzl 2009, pp.114-117. For a presentation of the doctrine of Dolpopa, see Stearns 1999). As for Tsongkhapa, his theory brings out an inert emptiness that resembles the second turning of the wheel presented previously, we will leave aside this theory. Dorji Wangchuk indicates based on Mipham that from the meditative standpoint, Dolpopa and Tsongkhapa agree – the highest reality is the absence of mental elaborations. Thus, according to Mipham, « both Dol-po-pa and Tsong-kha—pa, like many other Indian and Tibetan scholars and sages, were referring to one and the same absolute truth upon which ironically, both vehement disputes and reconciliation hinged », Wangchuk 2005, p.201.

391 It would be interesting to study these different wisdoms in comparison with the debates on pure consciousness. The following references investigate this question: Katz, 1978, Forman, 1990; Kapstein, 2004.

Conclusion

Two modes of knowledge

The wisdom of suchness and that of diversity characterize the cognition of a Buddha. How did they articulate themselves?

According to Jamgön Kongtrul Lodrö Thayé, phenomena appear as the center of space during meditation, and they are like an illusion during the subsequent attainment[392]. From then, we could think that the two forms of knowledge would appear at two different moments, but Jamgön Kongtrül Lodrö Thayé indicates that there is no distinction between these two moments:

> Although there are no distinctions between meditative equipoise and subsequent attainment in buddha wisdom, [the above two wisdoms] are labeled [in this way] merely due to [this buddha wisdom's two] ways of knowing[393]. NYC, *Luminous Heart*, p.292.

The terms "meditative absorption" (or "meditation") and "subsequent attainment" are not presented as an alternative between two distinct moments. Subsequent attainment does not lack the view on the suchness of phenomena, but it corresponds to the manifestation of suchness. Thus, the two wisdoms are non-distinct while also being non-identical[394], they are the two modes of knowing of a Buddha.

392 "These wisdoms can be summarized in the two categories of knowing suchness and knowing variety. As for the first, the nature of all phenomena—the ultimate lack of appearance—refers to the wisdom of knowing suchness in meditative equipoise. [...] The wisdom of knowing variety during subsequent attainment is the direct realization that all possible types of substances of all phenomena within the three times are illusion-like." NYC, in Luminous Heart, p.29. We can find the same thing in DDV (Maitreya 2004, p.156-157).

393 *De'ang sangs rgyas kyi ye shes la mnyam rjes ris su bcad pa med kyang mkhyen tshul tsam las btags pa'o/* Texte extrait du *rnam par shes pa dang ye shes 'byed pa'i bstan bcos kyi tshig don go gsal du 'grel pa rang byung dgongs pa'i rgyan*, [*[Jamgön Kongtrul Lodrö Tayé's commentary on NY]*], in *mdo sngags mtshams sbyor*, Volume 1 Pages 357 – 412.

394 The definition of meditative absorption and subsequent attainment can be different depending on the context (Arguillère 2007, pp.328-330 ; Arguillère 2008, p.210 ; 216).

Knowledge of the absolute

The description of the four wisdoms has shown that the notions of subject and object are completely modified at this stage. This is about a knowledge that has no subject-object duality[395]. Let's remember that the cause of illusion is grasping. The subject's grasping is characterized by the apprehension of a self that is permanent, unique, and independent; the grasping of an object is characterized by the apprehension of an object that is external to oneself, itself also permanent, unique, and independent. Without grasping, subject and object do not respond to these descriptions, but to those of the four wisdoms. The *dharmadhātu* summarizes the knowledge of the absolute.

> The three kāyas including their activities,
> Which are the changes of state of mind[396], mentation[397], and consciousness[398],
> Are perfected as the maṇḍala of the dharmadhātu[399] free from reference points. NY [156-158] in *Luminous Heart,* p.303.

In the *Vocabulaire du Bouddhisme,* the *dharmadhātu* is translated by "Real Element," and its definition used elements that were previously mentioned:

---

395 Stéphane Arguillère presents the three standpoints on the knowledge of the absolute particularly based on Tsongkhapa and Gorampa (Arguillère 2007, p.307 and s.).

396 The eighth consciousness disappears to leave space to mirrorlike wisdom.

397 The seventh consciousness – the afflicted mental – becomes the wisdom of equality.

398 The six consciousnesses become discriminating and all-accomplishing wisdom.

399 *Sems yid rnam shes gnas gyur pa'i/ sku gsum mdzad par bcas pa rnams/ chos dbyings spros bral dkyil 'khor du/ rdzogs pa*. Jamgön Kongtrul Lodrö Thayé uses the term "wisdom of the *dharmadhātu*" (NYC, [156-161]) whereas the 3rd Karmapa only uses the term "*dharmadhātu*." The distinction is important because in the Yogācāra, *chos dbyings* is not considered as a wisdom but only as a base (or cognitive object) of wisdom (see *The Ornament of the Mahāyāna* Sūtras, IX.67). In other words, there are only four wisdoms in *The Ornament of the Mahāyāna Sūtras* and the 3rd Karmapa is faithful to this presentation. Dolpopa and Shakya Chogdan, however, defend the idea that *chos dbyings* must be a wisdom. As for Rong zom Pandita (see Almogi 2007 and 2010), he refuses any cognitive element amidst the *chos dbyings.*

> The "Real Element," it's the sum of all things in the "three times" (past, present, future), as it is grasped in a non-dual and intemporal way by the principle-base knowledge of Buddhas. When all the implications of this definition are extracted, it appears that the ultimate nature of things is nothing else than Awakening itself of the Buddhas, since within the adequate perception, the opposition between object, or substance, and subject, or consciousness, cannot be maintained. Sharing the same essence of emptiness, all phenomena inter-penetrate each other and inter-express themselves. Emptiness does not abolish their individual characteristics, they are not indistinctly melted into one another, but maintained in the infinite richness of their detail. The *sūtra* describes each of them as the mirror of all the other ones, and of itself in them, and so on, in a vertiginous imagery that is, for us, the least inadequate metaphor of their reciprocal inherence. [...] Arguillère 2002 p.43-44[400].

All phenomena are amidst the same space, without duality, in an intemporal manner. The temporal aspect had been previously set aside during the presentation of discriminating wisdom. Jamgön Kongtrul Lodrö Thayé was describing it as being in the present moment (or in the instant)[401]. The "present moment" is also a key concept in the Mahāmudrā. The present moment should not be understood literally. First, the recognition of the nature of consciousness does not only consist in not being preoccupied by the past or the future, otherwise, it would boil down to staying at the level of instruction of the first Turning of the Wheel. Additionally, the present is refuted from the standpoint of the absolute:

> Time is this one instant,
> It does not come from another place. NT, Stanza 4 [15-16].
>
> The time of saṃsāra and nirvāṇa appearing and being mistaken as two is this very moment, it does not come via some place else, because all phenomena are dependent origination. NTC, Stanza 4, in *Luminous Heart* p.209

400 Other analyses on this term from other authors can be consulted: Arguillère 2002, p.81-94, Arguillère 2007, p.213 ; 332 ; 442.

401 Tib. *Skad gcig*.

The sentence "it does not come from another place" can be a reference to the past and the future. What we think to be time, a present that would come from the past to escape towards the future, is only, from the absolute standpoint, a succession of instants of presence without references. The grasping of the present in opposition to the past and the future is the fruit of a misunderstanding, time has no existence in itself. Therefore, being in the present as ordinary consciousness understands it does not free from the grasping of time.

The present moment cannot only be interpreted as being attentive in the present or enjoying the present. This understanding is a mechanism of ordinary consciousness. Additionally, according to Buddhism, the acquisition of a precious human existence is essential to realizing Awakening. This opportunity is considered as rare. If this existence is limited to enjoying the present moment in the ordinary sense of the term, the chance of deepening the true nature of reality is lost. Being in the present moment rather points to a presence to oneself, in a permanent way, that goes beyond any form of temporal structure and encompasses everything. This is a presence that is in direct contact with the raw matter of existence, time beyond the time, the intemporal. "The *dhātu* of time without beginning is the place of all phenomena."

Supreme Peace and Awakened Activity

The peace of phenomena's non-self

The *dharmadhātu* is also synonymous of great bliss[402]. The realization of the *dharmakāya* is synonymous to peace and well-being in itself[403]. There is therefore an intrinsic link between recognition of consciousness's nature and bliss[404].

The 3rd Karmapa does not express himself much on this question in the *Treatise on Pointing Out Buddha Nature*. He only mentions that the peace of arhats is not awakening:

---

402 Sct. *mahāsukha*, tib. *dbe ba chen po*. NTC, Stanza 13.

403 RGV I. 54/51, II. 34/164.

404 Also see RGV, I.37/ 35c, RGV, I. 54/51.

> [Awakening] is not similar to the peace of the *śrāvakas* and the *pratyekabouddhas*
> Because it displays all the qualities of formal bodies. Stanza 41 [192-193].

Rangjoung Dorje justifies his claim from the standpoint of qualities. In contrary to the arhats, the Buddhas realize the qualities of formal bodies (*saṃbhogakāya* et *nirmāṇakāya*), which necessarily implies a different awakening. The perception of a Buddha is richer and the source of vaster activity that deploys itself throughout the three *kāyas*. How can such perception also provide supreme peace?

Let's remember that the *arhat*'s peace cannot be perfect in the context that was previously presented. Indeed, the *arhat* seeks to escape from the *saṃsāra* to move towards the *nirvāṇa*. The *saṃsāra* must be avoided in order to access peace. Additionally, since this practice is not focused on the realization of phenomena's non-self, the practitioner remains amidst a subtle duality with the external world. Thus, peace is still conditioned, since one must be in a certain "place" to be at peace. Behind the remedies practiced by the *arhat* hides a fear of *saṃsāra*[405]. Yet, as soon as there is fear, there cannot be peace that is truly deep. The appeasement that this meditation provides certainly allows one to face the world with more serenity, but it is not enough to be at ease in every situation[406]. The realization which is reached does not have the means to face it.

However, the state of Buddhahood implies a non-differentiation between the *saṃsāra and the nirvāṇa*[407], since all phenomena have the same flavor. This is a characteristic that differentiates the *Mahāyāna* from the vehicle of foundation in general:

> Indian Māhāyana Buddhists minimized the opposition between nirvāṇa and saṃsāra, renouncing the suggestion that nirvāṇa was an escape from the world of suffering. Instead, they thought of enlightenment as a wise and compassionate way of living in that world. The adherents

405 See Limits of the *arhats*.

406 This realization does not encourage one either to come back from life to life to help beings, as it is the case for *bodhisattvas*. See § Awakened activity.

407 See Wisdom of Equality

> of the two major Indian branches of Māhāyana philosophy, Madhyamaka and Yogācāra, each developed their own way of rejecting the escapism to which, it was thought, the Abhidharma interpretation led. Thomas Kasulis, Nirvāṇa, *Encyclopedia of religion, vol.10,* p.6629.

Therefore, this implies that the *Buddhas* are not afraid of the *saṃsāra.* Since, for them, *saṃsāra* and *nirvāṇa* are not two distinct states, there is no saṃsāra that one should flee from. The experience in any situation can be mastered, there is nothing to adopt, nothing to reject. The literatures of the tantras would probably offer more elements to establish more precisely the link between the recognition of phenomena's nature and bliss.

Awakened activity, the three *kāyas*

The realization of emptiness is also associated with boundless compassion[408] and an activity said to be "awakened."

The activity of Buddhas is described through the three *kāyas* or three bodies[409] - *dharmakāya*[410], *saṃbhogakāya*[411] and *nirmāṇakāya*[412]. The *dharmakāya* accomplishes the benefits for oneself whereas the two other formal bodies (*saṃbhogakāya* and *nirmāṇakāya*) work for the beings deeply entrenched into *saṃsāra.* « Kāya » can be trans-

408 A couple of authors have looked into the link between emptiness and compassion in the context of *A Guide to the Bodhisattva's Way of Life* written by Śāntideva, especially regarding verses 101 à 103 of the eighth chapter. Let's also cite Williams Paul, *Studies in the Philosophy of the Bodhicaryāvatāra: Altruism and Reality*. Delhi, India: Motilal Banarsidass, 1998; Harris Stephen, *Does Anātman Rationally Entail Altruism? On Bodhicaryāvatāra 8:101-103*, Journal of Buddhist Ethics, Volume 18, 2011. Ludovic Viévard has also written a book on this subject with a larger perspective - *Vacuité (śūnyatā) et compassion (karunā) dans le bouddhisme Madhyamaka*, De Boccard, 2002.

409 For a detailed study of the different bodies, see Makransky John, *Buddhahood Embodied: Sources of Controversy in India and Tibet*, SUNY Series in Buddhist Studies, ed., Matthew Kapstein, Albany: SUNY Press, 1997.

410 Tib. *chos kyi sku.*

411 Tib. *longs spyod rdzogs pa'i sku.*

412 Tib. *sprul pa'i sku*. The four wisdoms are linked to the three *kāyas*. Mirrorlike wisdom is linked to the *dharmakāya*, wisdom of equality and discriminating wisdom are associated with the *sambhogakāya*, and all-accomplishing wisdom to *nirmāṇakāya*. Thus, the wisdoms that emerge from mirrorlike wisdom are linked to formal bodies.

lated by "body," but in this context, this is not about the physical body. This is more about a "base," a "substrate," or a "support" for all qualities[413] of consciousness, allowing different forms[414] to appear. The *saṃbhogakāya* is the activity resulting from the wisdom of equality and discriminating wisdom, it is in relation with speech. An awakened being continuously delivers the teachings of the dharma in the right place, the right time, and to the right person[415]. The *nirmāṇakāya* is the activity resulting from discriminating wisdom and all accomplishing wisdom, they are in relation with the physical body. An awakened being can permanently incarnate[416] to transmit the dharma in multiple ways[417]. How is such activity possible?

Let's first mention the faculties of a *buddha*. Through the realization of emptiness, any kind of dualism has vanished, there is only one space. The relationship to oneself and the world is vaster, deeper, and direct. A Buddha therefore perceives much more, and their capacity to feel is probably higher. Others' suffering is therefore more palpable[418]. Additionally, awakening 'implies the presence of multiple psychic powers, the bodies of qualities[419]. It will be easier for a buddha to develop multiple skillful means[420] in order to help all beings. This help aims to free all beings from *saṃsāra* – engaging in the world for the awakening of all beings is the sole motivation of a *Buddha*[421].

---

413 Sct. *dharma*, tib. *chos*.

414 Sct. *rūpa*, tib. *gzugs*.

415 The five certitudes of the saṃbhogakāya can be found in *The Ornament of the Mahāyāna Sūtras,* VIII.21.

416 « In terms of how they appear to beings, the continua of sambhogakāyas and nirmāṇakāyas are in themselves momentarily changing displays, and the mind streams of the beings who perceive them are momentarily changing as well. So, one aspect of the momentariness of the rūpakāyas is that their wisdom (especially its discriminating part) and their enlightened activities must entail movement and change in order to perceive countless different beings to be guided and perform beneficial functions for them. The other aspect is that, in order to be perceptible to the momentarily changing minds of beings, the rūpakāyas and their activities must be momentary too, because, by definition, it is not possible for a momentarily impermanent subject to perceive a permanent object » (Brunnhölzl 2009, note 600).

417 On the permanence of the three *kāyas*, see NT Stanza 37.

418 Tarthang Tulku 1977, ch.16.

419 See NT, Stanzas 14 and following.

420 Sct. *upāya*, tib. *thabs*.

421 In the case of ordinary consciousness, it is egotic desire that motivates the actions.

But why would this superior knowledge bring one to engage oneself for the sake of all beings, life after life? To free oneself and not fear *saṃsāra* does not necessarily imply the will to stay for others forever. Couldn't we imagine being conscious of others' suffering and trying to remediate to it without wishing to come back again and again in *saṃsāra?* On the path, the advice is to take on the vows of a *bodhisattva* in which one vows to free all brings from suffering[422]. Consequently, other factors seem necessary to accomplishing an activity for the benefit of others. One must engage, wish, and train until qualities such as generosity or patience are perfectly accomplished. Besides, it seems that engaging for others simultaneously leads to benefits for oneself. The opening towards others forces us to push our limits further. Finally, perhaps this motivation is necessary for our own liberation.

Jamgön Kongtrül Lodrö Thayé explains that the activity of a *Buddha* is love, knowledge, and power[423]. This activity is the result of the victorious ones' benediction, the wishes, and it can get in contact with the beings possessing a pure *karma*. By reading this sentence, it seems that a *Buddha* could act directly on the manifestation, in accords with the wish and disposition of all beings[424]. Due to non-dual perception and the wishes, some kind of "inevitable meetings" can occur. Besides, what needs to be understood by pure *karma*? The *karma* is by definition always impure, because it is the fruit of egocentric actions. Purity, in this context, can be partly explained by good actions, also called "merit," accumulated by a being, which allow to find again an "opening" to receive, meet.

Being inconceivable, awakened activity is compared to a jewel able to fulfill all wishes[425].

---

422 Gampopa 1999, chapter 9 and following. In certain cases, it is also indicated that the *Buddha* comes to "awaken" the *arhats* who think that they have reached the supreme *nirvāṇa*, Gampopa 1998, chapter 1, p.52-53.

423 NT, Stanza 31 and see also RGV I.31/30 in which compassion is compared to water.

424 Also see RGV, IV.1-2/215-216.

425 The *Supreme Continuum insurpassable* gives eight other examples to illustrate this activity, see RGV IV, 13-98/224-278.

Why all Beings are Buddhas

Following the previous developments, the two questions that were first asked in the general introduction can now be reintroduced: "How to understand that everything is already there?", and "how to recognize directly the nature of consciousness?"

Presence of Buddha Nature in all beings

Ordinary consciousness and awakened consciousness are two very distinct modes of consciousness. Yet, the text unceasingly claims that they have a common basis. They are not completely different, but they cannot be completely identical either, otherwise awakened consciousness would not be awakened anymore, or ordinary consciousness would not be ordinary anymore.

Evolution of perception over the three turnings

By studying the perception of ordinary consciousness, experience revealed itself as very shrunk, compact, regulated, and frozen by the *saṃskāras.* The experience of the arhat is much more flexible, since they are not trapped by perceived objects anymore, and they realized the individual no-self. However, they are still in a form of duality. Finally, Buddhas presents themselves as a being that is in an opening without references, in which emptiness and luminosity are in union.

In the three cases, we are talking about a stream of consciousness, a sequence of instants of knowing. The difference lies in the subject-object relationship. Ordinary consciousness is in a very tight relationship in which subjects and objects are over-determined. An *arhat* recognizes the non-self of the subject but remains in ignorance regarding the perceived object and the true nature of the subject. A *Buddha* denies both subject and object, and elevates themselves to a level of perception that is without any mental elaboration. These descriptions and the exercises of meditation show that the subject-object duality is more or less tight depending on the capacity to insert space within perception. In the ordinary case, the perception is completely buried in or dominated by the *saṃskāras.* There is no resting moment, everything is interpreted quickly and systematically depending on the framework of interpretation shaped by previous experiences. Through the practices linked to the first turning, some space is "created," or rather freed up, within perception. Then, going beyond the state of arhat is done thanks to meditative exercises that lead towards the body-space and the consciousness-space. Thus, depending on each case, the space is more or less vast. An instant of consciousness can be perceived either with a very large vision, either with a very narrow vision – both within presence to oneself and presence to the world. This is the same stream of consciousness, which, while awakening, is likened to some sort of dilation. Dualistic grasping compresses and limits consciousness, space dilate and opens towards the infinite. A parallel can be established with the formation of the universe, in which a process of solidification appears:

> Earth rests upon water and water upon wind.
> Wind fully rests on space.
> Space does not rest upon any of the elements
> of wind, water, or earth[426]. *Buddha Nature,* p.26.

426 According to ancient Indian cosmology used by Buddhism, the universe's formation is thought starting from space, with the successive appearance of the wind, water, and then earth. The formation of our world is also compared to the formation of the universe. Beings appear and disappear, following the same laws as the external world does. The element of fire is not mentioned, because it is used to illustrate illness, aging, and death, which destroys our existence. (Brunnhölzl 2014, note 1330 p.1088).

The space

Establishing the recognition of space as a characteristic of a consciousness's level of awakening sheds light on the meaning of the universal presence of Buddha Nature. Indeed, space is not something private or reserved only to a few people. Space is everywhere, it is permanent, and makes no distinction. If we know how to get in contact with it, it will always be available to us.

> *Buddhas* are like space,
> And ordinary beings have the same characteristics. NT, Stanza 47 [209-210].

In the *Supreme Continuum* and the *Treatise on Pointing Out Buddha Nature*, the *dhātu* is often compared to space through different perspectives. Like space, the dhātu is omnipresent and without concept[427]. Jamgön Kongtrül Lodrö Thayé takes the example of three receptacles[428]. The first one is of clay, the second one of copper, and the third of gold. They represent respectively ordinary beings, *bodhisattvas*, and *buddhas*. Even if the three receptacles are not made of the same material, the space within them is identical. Whichever level of consciousness, the infinite space is always at the bottom. Besides, just like phenomena could not appear if they did not have space as basis[429], phenomena could not appear if they were not emptiness. From this space, or emptiness, will arise the different elements, then the forms and the mental events. Even if it is not perceived anymore, space will always be at the source. This comparison to space also provides an illustration of why the *dhātu* cannot be affected by impurity. In space, the different worlds manifest themselves, remain for some time, and then disintegrate. Despite these events, space itself does not change[430]. It is the same thing for the *dhātu*. Whatever type of manifestation arises within it, it will never be affected. Even when the consciousness seems

427 RGV I. 49/46.

428 *Buddha Nature. The Mahāyāna Uttaratantra shastra with commentary* 2000, p.129.

429 RGV I.55/52. Used by Jamgön Kongtrül Lodrö Thayé in the commentary of stanzas 2 and 10 of the *Treatise on Pointing Out Buddha Nature.*

430 RGV I. 54/51.

impure, the *dhātu* is never stained[431]. Impure thoughts can emanate from purity, and these do not alter at all the immaculate nature of consciousness itself, because its nature is permanent, non-dependent of causes and conditions. It cannot be degraded by ordinary beings trapped in confusion, and it cannot be improved either by the vision of the wises[432]. Consciousness' nature is comparable to space, but depending on the modes of being, space is more or less restricted. Everything is located in space and is constituted of space, however, access to the latter depends on the grasping of *saṃskāras.*

The qualities are indissociable from the nature of consciousness

Space is not empty. It can welcome everything, but it is not only a "passive" receptacle. The *dhātu* is also inseparable from their countless qualities[433]. The *Supreme Continuum* compares this relationship between space and qualities with the sun and its rays:

> Its qualities are inseparable, like the sun and its rays[434].
> *Buddha Nature, p.30*
> Illuminating, radiating, and purifying,
> and inseparable from each other, analytical wisdom,
> primordial wisdom, and total liberation
> correspond to the light, rays, and orb of the sun[435]. Ibid., p.31.

431 NT, Stanza 7.

432 NT, Stanza 13. Longchenpa's works offer a much deeper analysis of the relationship of phenomena with the *dharmadhātu* : "Klong-chen rab-'byams, inspired by the literature of the *rDzogs-chen*, was interested more than any other Tibetan author by the immanent production of content from Awakening as auto-manifestation of essence on one hand, and on the other, to the modalities according to which the production of *saṃsāra* relates to this pure expression of Reality." Arguillère 2007, p.335. In the *Profusion de la vaste sphere,* the different theses on this topic are developed (pp.334 et s.).

433 « Naturally pure and consistent with permanent qualities » (NT, Stanza 1 [2]) ; NT Stanza 19 ; RGV I. 155/134. The fire of wisdom burns the defilement, but the luminosity of consciousness doesn't (*Hymn to the dharmadhātu,* Stanza 20 (Brunnhölzl 2007, p.231). These qualities are established spontaneously, and they are not determined. See Arguillère 2007, pp.347-356; p.385.

434 *De phyir nyi dang zer bzhin yon tan dbyer med pas/*

435 *Shes rab ye shes rnam grol rnams/ gsal dang 'phro dang dag phyir dang/ tha dad med phyir 'od dang zer/ nyi ma'i dkyil 'khor rnams dang mtshungs/*

The *dhātu*, creator

In Stanza 5 of the *Treatise on Pointing Out Buddha Nature*, the *dhātu* is expressed as a creator because of its characteristics, without truly being one[436]. The *dhātu* is a creator[437] in the sense that it possesses all the qualities[438], but if the *dhātu* already possesses these qualities, this means that it does not create them.

Yet, when they manifest, they seem to be created, which is why the *dhātu* is a creator without being one. Even if the qualities seem indeed produced or new, since consciousness did not experience them before, it is in reality only an unveiling of what is already present, there is nothing to add[439]. The qualities are therefore completely present and permanent, they are indissociable from the nature of consciousness, just like the sun is indissociable from its rays[440].

---

436 NT, Stanza 5.

437 Tib. *byed po*.

438 NTC, Stanza 5.

439 We find again this principle in the translation of the term "Buddha," in Tibetan "*sangs rgyas*." *Sangs* means "to purify" and *rgyas* "to blossom."

440 Not everyone agrees on the status of the qualities. As for the qualities attributed to the different *kāyas*, there is no debate. However, two questions are asked about these. Are all or only certain qualities present in the ordinary state? Additionally, do they exist in a subtle or complete way (see Mathes 2008, p.3)? Regarding the first question, Rangjung Dorje does not adopt the same position depending on the context. In the context of the Mahāyāna tradition, only the qualities of the *dharmakāya* are present (ordinary approach), whereas in the context of the Vajrayāna, all qualities are present (extraordinary approach) - Mathes 2008, p.71-72. The 3rd Karmapa does not seem to explain why the qualities of the *rūpakāya* are already present in the context of the Vajrayāna tradition only. Regarding the second question, Rangjung Dorje explicitly writes several times that the qualities have been present in a complete way forever (NT Stanzas 1, 2, 5, 13 ...). Additionally, the example of the statue in gold used in the *Treatise on Pointing Out Buddha Nature* can also be an indication that the 3rd Karmapa supports the complete presence of Buddhahood's qualities. Indeed, the sixth and eighth examples, the seed of a fruit and the ugly lady bearing the protector of men, suggests a gradual development of the qualities, whereas the statue in gold covered with defilements suggests that they do not have to mature (See Zimmermann 2002, p.62-65). However, this permanent presence is not substantial. To avoid wrong interpretations, Zhönu Pal offers to qualify this presence as "subtle" (Mathes 2008, chapitre 5). They are here, but under a specific mode. At first sight, these questions on the qualities seem artificial, since they are inconceivable. Why then debate whether they are complete, subtle or absent, and specify which ones are the qualities that are already present ? The question related to these controversies seems to be the following: are the qualities created dependant on certain conditions or are they inherent to emptiness? If the qualities are not complete but only present under the form of seeds, then it is necessary to reunite different causes and conditions

Causality of the transformation

The qualities are unveiled and not created, like the purification of the beryl. It is only about removing the different depositions that have been accumulated on the gem. From then, a change of state[441] happens. We could also talk about a "transformation" of the experience:

> The path is seen as the progressive clarification and refinement of what has been there all along, primordial knowing or buddha nature. Here 'transformation' is used figuratively, the salient insight being that spiritual refinement, like the refinement of gold, does not change what is sought (i.e. one's natural condition, gold) but only removes all that it is not so as to allow it to be progressively revealed. Higgins 2012, p.250.

If the term of "transformation" is chosen, it would be more appropriate to understand it as a "change of state," a passage from form to non-form.

It is indicated that the *dhātu* expresses, first of all, a causal sense[442]. In other words, thanks to its presence, a change of state is possible for all beings. However, this is not a cause that produces an effect. If it was the case, this would imply that the *dhātu* is neither unconditional, nor permanent, since the ordinary cause-to-effect relationship leads to a dependence between the two – the cause must modify itself to give birth to the effect. The space is once again called onto to illustrate the causality that is the current focus:

so that they can develop. If this is the case, awakening cannot be unconditional. Yet, the texts on Buddhahood indeed specify that the absolute is not dependent on causes and conditions. Additionally, if the qualities are conditioned, awakening cannot be stable, since it would be dependent on causes and conditions, which is to say on external conditions. If this is the case, several consequences would ensue: suffering can come back; phenomena would not have a uniform and homogeneous flavor; consciousness will not be the absolute refuge – consciousness would therefore not be a foundation onto which we could rest in any circumstance. Each of these consequences is due to conditioning. Therefore, in order for awakening to be unconditioned, the qualities necessarily have to be already present and permanent.

441 tib. *gnas 'gyur*. Stéphane Arguillère also offers the term of "transfiguration," Arguillère 2007, p. 305.

442 NTC, Stanza 5.

Space is not a cause, and yet the cause
for all visible things to be seen,
for sound, odor, flavor, touch,
and phenomena to be heard and so on[443]. *Buddha Nature* p.47.

The *dhātu* is a cause, in the sense that the qualities of awakening appear naturally once the veils are purified, because they are not overshadowed anymore. Therefore, the causes of the qualities would actually be what eradicates their respective veils – a specific cause purifies a specific veil, this way letting show the quality that was, until now, recovered by a veil. Thus, the qualities are not coming from nowhere, they are not random. Certain causes must be set into place in order for them to blossom. The qualities are not created, and they appear according to a very specific process.

How to explain the presence of these qualities ?

As opposed to space that is more palpable, the presence of these countless qualities described from stanza 14 is less easy to apprehend. Nonetheless, the process of purification of afflictions can shed some light on this subject. Each affliction modifies perception, sometimes to the point of completely depriving it from discernment. For example, ordinary anger can blind and lead to actions that one regrets once the situation is appeased. But we can also observe that anger has qualities, it can be well-meaning or even offer great clarity. These qualities are, however, truly "visible" or "efficient" as soon as there is no more grasping. This reasoning could be applied on all afflictions, each of them encompassing its own qualities[444].

Regarding the other countless qualities of the *kāyas*, their presence can only be an object of trust. The afflictions and their "transformation" are easy to observe because of their gross character; however, the countless qualities of Buddhahood are perceived only

443 *Ji ltar rgyu min nam mkha' ni/ gzugs mthong ba dang sgra dang dri/ ro dang reg dang chos rnams ni/ thos la sogs pa'i rgyu yin ltar/*

444 On this subject, see the "Five families of Buddhas." Chögyam Trungpa offers a vivid description in *Journey without Goal: The Tantric Wisdom of the Buddha*, Shambala, 2000.

by *Buddhas*. None of the other beings – including the *bodhisattvas* – have access to it[445]. By admitting that they exist, the different qualities can only be unveiled throughout the practice:

> If this element[446] exists, through our work,
> We will see the purest of all gold.
> Without this element, despite our toil,
> Nothing but misery we will produce. *In Praise of Dharmadhātu*, Stanza 11, p.223

If the *dhātu* is really present and the practice of purifying the veils is correctly carried out, some experiences or qualities should arise. After a meditation session, numerous studies show that most of the time, one's relationship to one's body and consciousness is different. If a difference is noticed after a meditative practice, a retreat, why wouldn't it be possible to go even further? But until we access this view, that of pure gold, the *dhātu* remain an object of trust and point to the ultimate goal to realize. The realization of awakening "conditions" all the teaching of the *Buddha*, his analyses, and the offered path. Awakening is a principle that can be found again if the path is walked.

"We are not certain"

Yet, in the *Treatise on Pointing Out Buddha Nature*, the 3rd Karmapa writes that one must be certain of the absolute:

> Currently, we are going in the opposite direction of [these qualities].
> Because we are not certain of what is, just as it is
> We produce an imaginary world that thinks existing beings, which [actually] do not exist. NT, Stanza 18 [78-80].

445 RGV, V.I/ 279b.

446 *Dhātu*.

How to understand the term "certainty" within a thought that denies any true (or real) foundation of knowledge and whose goal is ineffable? How could we develop a certitude about the qualities of consciousness?

The notion of "certitude" implies the idea of a firm adhesion, where something is held as true, without any reserve. The certitude cannot be of a purely intellectual order, otherwise we would fall in the negative effects evoked in the Second Turning[447]. Only being confident that the qualities are indeed present does not seem enough to their unveiling either, since it would only be about a "superficial idea." In order for the certitude to be a factor of awakening, it must permit the opening of consciousness towards what really is[448]. In other words, certitude must be an "active principle" and not only an objective knowledge. Seeing the mechanism of afflictions changing state can generate a certitude, which will allow to turn away from the *saṃsāra. Regarding the other qualities, this certitude will necessarily be tainted with trust*[449]. At least, being certain that the purification process brings closer to what really is, is a first step. As soon as consciousness is in an ordinary attitude, the certitude is a reminder that leads consciousness to change its way of being – within each veil hides a quality.

Buddha Nature and Mahāmudrā

Buddha Nature is the basis of the Mahāmudrā practice. After briefly going over two expressions that are characteristic of the Mahāmudrā's essence, certain conditions will appear for the practice to be fertile.

447 Intellectual understanding eradicates gross ignorance only, consciousness would condemn itself to stay in the *saṃsāra*, regardless of how erudite it is.

448 J. Pettit qualifies the certitude of "causal connection" based on the *Beacon of Certainty* from Mipham: "In the Beacon, certainty (*nges shes*) mediates the causal connection between theory (*lta ba* in the critical philosophical context) and Gnostic vision (*lta ba* as experience that is the result of successful practice)", Pettit 1999, Introduction - Dialectical philosophy and the Great Perfection. Certitudes provides the link between reflection and meditation.

449 See notes on the different types of trust, NT Stanza 49.

Mahāmudrā's essence

"There is absolutely nothing to remove, Neither anything to add[450]" – the meaning of Buddha Nature is summarized here. The importance of this sentence has already been emphasized. If this affirmation is understood literally, we could deduce that there's nothing to do. This seems unlikely, due to the work that consciousness must accomplish to recognize its true nature[451]. "Neither anything to add" means that Buddha Nature is non-empty of its qualities that are inseparable. All qualities are already here[452]. "There is absolutely nothing to remove" means that Buddha Nature is empty of adventitious defilement. These defilements do not belong to Buddha Nature, and they cannot affect it, therefore, nothing is to be removed, the absolute is perfect[453]. Consequently, this key passage must be understood from the standpoint of the absolute. In order for awakening to reveal itself, it is very necessary to engage in a purification work that will allow the dissolution of defilements and the manifestation of qualities.

Natural consciousness[454], another key term of the Mahāmudrā, points to "non-conceptual wisdom." Just as the expression "There is absolutely nothing to remove, Neither anything to add", this term can lead, if understood literally, to simplifying interpretations such as "one must not think," "there is nothing to do." Yet, the descriptions of non-conceptual wisdom clearly challenge all literal understanding. Wisdom is not an absence of thoughts or an intellectual understanding. Therefore, meditation must go beyond analysis and does not consist in suppressing thoughts, otherwise the object of negation is not clearly identified. Indeed, it is not a certain thought or Thought in itself that must be negated, but the grasping of thought. Therefore, all the process that led to this thought is targeted, a thought is not detached from the context in which it arises. This is a complex process. Additionally, by trying to voluntarily suppress thoughts, there is always a duality – an "I" that tries to suppress the

450 NT, Stanza 19 [91-92].

451 On the question of the path without progression or without effort, see Higgins 2012. p.251-259.

452 Mathes 2008, p.330 ; Brunnhölzl 2014, p.901 et s.

453 See Brunnhölzl 2014, p.901 and following, Mathes 2008, p. 326-332.

454 Tib. *tha mal gyi shes pa.*

thoughts. There is the effort of the grasping self, of a self that does not want to think anymore, as subtle as it is. In doing so, one abandons discernment of the true nature of all phenomena, which can lead to scruffiness or falling back onto a primal anti-intellectualism in which no wisdom can arise from. The recognition of the nature of thought is a deep work that encompasses the totality of experience. When it comes to being "free from mental elaborations," the whole process of perception is challenged, from sensation (and even beyond that) to gross thoughts. Everything that contributes to grasping onto the representations of the world is put into question.

Following the explanations given regarding the meaning of "There is absolutely nothing to remove, Neither anything to add" and of natural consciousness, it appears that the terms linked to the direct Mahāmudrā practice implies a profound understanding of the mechanism of the ordinary self's deconstruction. Consequently, if the direct instructions are practiced without a consciousness of this deconstruction, the fruits cannot be reached, the illusion remains. The risk would then be to fall into the wrong interpretations of non-conceptual wisdom previously described. Intellectually understanding that everything is emptiness, that consciousness is non-born, or applying the instructions without true understanding is like replacing the grasping of a thought with another[455]. It is still the game of ordinary consciousness, because the practitioner does not know how to uproot the mechanisms of the self. Yet, the true self manifests itself naturally and consecutively to the deconstruction of dualistic grasping, it is not a conscious decision. It is possible to hypothesize that some experiences could manifest even without adequate understanding. However, we can question the sustainable aspect of these experiences or the capacity to renew them in order to stabilize them.

Even if Buddha Nature is present with all its qualities, it is still necessary to "obtain" it[456]. This term shows that some efforts must be furnished to be able to reach the desired fruit, because ignorant imagination covers up what is authentic. If the disciple does not

455 See example given by Śāntideva, previously cited. Instead of grasping onto existence, the practitioner will grasp onto non-existence; or instead of grasping onto ordinary ego, they will grasp onto a new ego based on the idea of being a *Buddha*. In the two cases, *dualistic* functioning is not transformed, because understanding remains mental, and confusion can even be greater.

456 Tib. *thob pa*. See NT Stanza 2.

have faculties that are sharpened enough to follow the direct way, they must opt for a gradual way. This claim is often found in the texts. For example, Gampopa writes that the direct way it's not appropriate for beginners, the beginners can only engage on the paths of the *pāramitās* and *mantras*[457]."

Gradual Way

The gradual path has already been touched on within the description of the three Turnings of the Wheel. Only two principles are presented here.

Deepening of experience

The concept of "*nirvāṇa*" could make one think that one leaves the *saṃsāra* for another place. Ordinary consciousness being used to objectify, the path could then be seen as a means to reach another state in the future. Consciousness would then move from point A to point B, searching for a place where it could be at peace. But this cannot be the case. If the *nirvāṇa* was a specific place (other than the place of rest within consciousness itself), it would then be

---

457 Mathes, 2008, p.41. We also find this idea in *Moonbeams*: « This Dakpo practice lineage contains both instructional traditions: One is taught for the instantaneous type, who first eliminate their misinterpretations concerning the ground and root and are then taught the techniques for resting in that [ground]. The other is provided for the gradual type, who first pursue mental stillness and then are led to vipaśyanā gradually. Although these days most people, being of the type that has a very clear and active mind, would at this point be more appropriately guided according to the first approach, here I will give the explanation according to the latter approach in consideration of what is better known at the moment ». *Moonbeams*, p.177. Kamalaśīla claims that the gradual way is a necessary passage towards non-conceptual wisdom in order to avoid stupidity: "In one of his works, Kamalaśīla considers the non-thought and the refusal of acquiring merits as a rejection of the Great Vehicle as a whole. The non-thought, it is "thinking about nothing," and as a result, rejecting wisdom whose characteristic is correct analysis. The latter being the root of correct wisdom, it is also a rejection of supra-mundane wisdom and "the main instrument of illumination called the discernment of the *dharma*." According to Kamalaśīla, it is impossible to penetrate the Absence of concept – which constitutes the *nirvāṇa* – without correct analysis, and without it, it is also impossible to practice the absence of memory and absence of reflection. Giving oneself to these practices without correct analysis, it is practicing stupidity. It is through the light of correct analysis that the "Yogin appeases in themselves all mental development; penetrates the knowledge exempt from context. Through the acquisition of this knowledge, they directly know emptiness." Mala 1985, p.398.

conditioned. Yet, the texts specify that awakening is unconditioned. Certain conditions are necessary for practice, but the aiming is indeed an unconditioned peace. In reality, *saṃsāra* and *nirvāṇa* are only conventional linguistic designations, they do not escape the critique of emptiness[458]. The *saṃsāra* corresponds to illusory tendencies, and Buddhahood does not designate anything in itself, only the lively and dynamic nature of consciousness that is available in each moment. Therefore, the change of state takes place in the same place, which is to say, consciousness. The path is the deepening of the now, of what is here. Consciousness does not awaken by jumping from *saṃsāra* to *nirvāṇa*, since there is no *saṃsāra* to leave to reach a peaceful place without suffering, otherwise, duality would remain, with a subject wishing to reach something. Consciousness must work on its own outlook by removing the different defilements that cover its true nature. It is not possible to "go seek" what is here or to create the qualities – the mechanisms of experience are to be understood. Only the outlook of the subject changes. The absolute is unconditioned and consequently never changes –it is perfect. "To change" only expresses the liberation of impurities[459].

Deactivating the process of grasping

The second principle raised is the "deactivation of grasping." Indeed, the 3rd Karmapa Rangjung Dorje mentions that the only difference between an ordinary being and an awakening being is the presence or absence of grasping[460]. Ordinary consciousness lives in dualistic grasping and bases its actions on the three poisons, whereas awakened consciousness lives in non-duality and bases its actions on the *bodhicitta*. With grasping, it's *saṃsāra*, without grasping, it's *nirvāṇa*. All the proposed practices on the path have as only and unique goal to relax what is contracted and thus open consciousness more and more. For example, it is written that the first five *pāramitās* allow for the accumulation of merit. One could also say that they enlarge space within experience because each of

458 NT Stanza 9, NTC, Stanza 4.

459 NT, Stanza 26 [127-136]. On the interpretations of "gnas 'gyur" which is to say, "change of state," see Higgins 2012, p.141-143.

460 NT Stanza 30.

them aims to lessen the grip of the "I." As for the *pāramitā* of wisdom, it gives sight. It is compared to a guide that accompanies us along the path.

Conclusion

By following these principles of purification, consciousness can let go of a world where mental elaborations rule and thus can recover a simple and clear perception. By following the progression of a gradual path, a true letting go is possible since the cogs of existence are understood. There is no objective to reach, there is nothing to suppress or manipulate. It is enough to only observe the movements related to experience and have a penetrating sight to avoid being caught in the nets of confusion. At the end of this progressive work, the emptiness-luminosity is not only an idea anymore, but it is integrated and understood from the inside. It is lived. We then avoid the creation of a new representation of the world that would be more "divine," and we are not prisoners of the terminology linked to the view and to the instructions of meditation. By treating the different aspects of grasping thanks to the gradual path, consciousness will then have the capacity to link itself directly to what it truly is.

The gradual path necessitates many more diverse instructions and teachings, which one must think about and meditate on. Then, gradually, new habits will settle in, allowing one to get closer to the nature of consciousness, until the moment when no more instruction is necessary. Indeed, once the exercise becomes familiar, the path to walk becomes clearer, and so does the "result" where the path wants to bring us.

At this stage, consciousness can then settle or land on this understanding and see in a direct way[461]. One can then observe that the

461 Buddhahood is characterized by a purity that is beyond purity and impurity, beyond any mental elaboration, and the direct path is at this level, that of the fruit. However, the gradual way consists in walking the path by following the different *pāramitās*. We then speak of a "causal" way. Yet, "virtue does not mislead less often than vice does, just as white clouds do not obscure the sky less often than black clouds do. The rejected illusion is that which would consist to believe, precisely, that it is about *producing* the fruit of Awakening thanks to the multiple aspects of the Path" (Arguillère 2007, p.461). This opposition between the two ways is also found in what Paul Démiéville describes regarding the doctrines proposed by Houei-neng and Chen-sieou : " Philosophically, the two doctrines are based, one just like

two ways can be complementary. Taking side for one or the other position would not reflect the complexity of the Buddhist path[462]. Even if the means are different, the gradual path of the *pāramitās* has the same goal as the Mahāmudrā of essence: realizing natural consciousness[463].

Let's note moreover that the direct path cannot be the equivalent of the realization of perfect awakening. Perfect awakening corresponds, we have seen it, to the realization of the four wisdoms and the three *kāyas* – all defilements have been purified. As for the direct path, it is first of all cultivating a way of knowing that does not rely on mental representations anymore. Therefore, even in the case of a direct or a simultaneous meditation, the realization of

the other, on the belief in the purity itself of the mind ; but pure by nature, the mind is defiled by the "adventitious passions." Gradualism insists on the necessary effort to rid the mind from foreign impurities, to "wipe and scrub the mirror" ; subitism only wants to take into account its essential purity, to the point of refusing to recognize the existence of impurity, even to get rid of it : the distinction between purity and impurity already implies, indeed, a dualism, a relativism that is contrary to the unpredictability of the absolute, which itself is "empty" of any determination. If Buddha-nature (*fo-sing*, the *buddhatā*, the virtual capacity to become Buddhas that is innate to all beings and by which they participate powerfully to all Buddhas' nature, which is an absolute and pure essence), if the absolute, because it is one of its names, is "eternally pure," it is not in the sense that it differs from the impure, from dust: it is identity in itself." Démiéville 1973, p.134 (our own translation). One of the challenges of the gradual path is therefore to know how to operate the transition between causal approach and approach through the fruit (see Higgins 2012, p.259).

462 D. Higgins emphasizes that the first authors of the Dzogchen considered the gradual alternative /direct caricatural (Higgins 2012, p.227). Let's note that this opposition was perhaps not as solidified between the two Chinese Masters: "As if emphasized, at the beginning of the *Platform Sūtra,* which, in the complete title of its most ancient review, appears like a presentation of the "sudden doctrine" (*touen-kiao*), these stanzas oppose this doctrine, that of Houei-neng, and the "gradual doctrine" (*tsien-kiao*) which was that of Chen-sieou. It is not certain, in reality, that the doctrinal opposition between these two masters was truly cut and dry, perhaps was it more like a tradition which must come after them." Démiéville 1973, p.133 (our own translation).

463 Jigten Sumgön ('Jig rten gsum mgon) writes that "all the Turnings of the Wheel are contained in each Turning" Mathes, 2008, p. 42. In reality, there is only one vehicle: "Considered in light of the progressive broadening of the aspirant's moral/spiritual horizons in the transformations from individualism (Hīnayāna) to altruism (Mahayāna) to pure perception (Vajrayāna), the spiritual vehicles and their ethical disciplines reflect crucial milestones or phase-transitions along a single path". Higgins 2012, p.249-250. The joint presence of the gradual and direct paths within the *Treatise On Pointing Out Buddha Nature* contrasts with what is usually presented to us in the debate of Samyé (See Démiéville, 1987 ; Ruegg 1989 ; Arguillère 2007, pp.444-456) or even in the opposition between Houei-neng and Chen-sieou (See Paul Démiéville, *Le miroir spirituel*, 1973), where the two paths seem to constitute two alternatives that mutually exclude each other.

perfect awakening can probably not be immediate, the complete recognition of Buddha Nature remains gradual.

We can hypothesize that there is especially a difference in attitude towards *karma* that arises. In ordinary state, the *karma* is reaffirmed, because consciousness only follows the footprints that generated it. By applying the antidotes, white tendencies accumulate,[464] which allows the generation of positive karma, but this remains conditioned. With a direct approach, the *karma* – whether positive or negative – dissolves, because it is recognized. Without black or white samskaric reaction, the karmic trace dissolves. The practice consists then in stabilizing oneself in what has been seen directly, and never become distracted from it, regardless of circumstances, until all *karma* is purified. Therefore, even if the method is direct, it does not seem to have the capacity to purify in one instant all of the accumulated *karma.* These are two distinct processes. Everything that is "contained" in the *ālayavijñāna* manifests itself one day or the other when the causes and conditions are brought together, and with each manifestation of the tendencies that were buried until then, the direct method is to be applied. The meditative practice does not mainly focus on the contents of experience, but on the shape of experience. In other terms, there would be two types of unconsciousness – the unconsciousness of dualistic grasping (the seventh consciousness, named "afflicted mental"), and the unconsciousness linked to our "experiences of life" (the eighth consciousness).

The coemergence

Direct perception leads us again to the notion of coemergence, another key term presented in the introduction: from one unique foundation can arise two modes of consciousness. The practice of the Mahāmudrā invites us to perceive the absolute dimension in each phenomenon. Indeed, whatever the phenomenon, the absolute dimension is always present with it. Jamgön Kongtrul Lodrö Thayé explains that purity and impurity are intermingled, they are not separate[465]. Therefore, when consciousness is influenced by *karma* or af-

464 NTC, Stanza 6.
465 NTC, Stanza 2.

flictions, it does not cut itself away from its true nature. He takes the example of muddy water, in which soil and water are mixed up, to show that confusion is never separate from wisdom, they are together[466]. In the ordinary case, water presents itself under the form of ice, and space is reduced to the views of consciousness. In the awakened case, water is clear, fluid, and space is open and vast. Despite the different manifestations of one and the other, water and space have the same nature in the two cases. Saraha compare is this to two trunks that can come from the same seed[467].

Either consciousness does not recognize itself[468] and engages itself in the grasping of a self, thus creating *saṃsāra*; either consciousness recognizes its true nature and rests in wisdom and peace. By affirming the permanent presence of emptiness-luminosity, this principle of recognition makes sense. Indeed, if one had to fabricate luminosity or create it, a direct recognition would not be possible. Therefore, the teachings on Buddha Nature establish and justify the practice of the Mahāmudrā. The fruit being already present, the practitioner can practice recognizing it from now, from the beginning:

> Thus, every samsaric state of mind, can be the starting point of Mahāmudrā, even the wildest forms of defilement can be experienced as the perfection of purity, bliss and the like by simply abiding and relaxing within them and calming down. The qualities of the buddha nature are not something other than or somewhere else than in defilements. Mathes 2008, p.403.

Even amidst the wildest defilements, the nature of consciousness can then be touched, thanks to the meditation instructions. Thus, instead of considering such defilements as clouds covering the sky, they can be compared to a rainbow, the sun, or even the stars, that, far from obscuring the sky, illustrate it[469]."

---

466 Tib. *lhan cig*.

467 Mathes 2008, p. 259 (DRSM, 51.16-7).

468 It is then in ignorance (Tib. *ma rig pa*).

469 Arguillère 2007, p.215. « The true absolute is illustrated by the curious image of the sky completely empty, infused with luminous fog and « intangible « or « untactile « from appearances. The fog, here, is not conceived as a veil, as an occulting element; it is important to see that it is in itself the expression of the empty sky." Arguillère 2007, p.297 (our own translation).

Inseparability of the base and the fruit is key[470]. The objective is linking oneself directly to the nature of consciousness and its qualities, which is to say the fruit. Once the path towards the fundamental nature of consciousness is recognized and understood, it is possible to meditate and stabilize oneself directly within it[471]. Remembering that we are a *Buddha* allows us to cultivate a pure vision, and, this way, to pierce the veils until total exhaustion. Pure vision is important because as soon as consciousness solidifies a mental event, this understanding is a good reminder to dissolve that which, in ordinary anytime, freezes and settles[472]. The absolute reveals itself depending on the intensity of presence. Given that the nature of consciousness is always present, it is possible at any moment to find it again, to experience it, and thereby free ourselves of everything that restrains us. The *view* on Buddhahood allows the eradication of all views and leads us towards the Self[473].

---

470 See *Aspiration Prayer of Mahāmudrā of Definitive Meaning*, 1995 p.51-61.

471 This conclusion can also be found in the following extract from *The Philosophical Foundations of Classical rDzogs chen in Tibet* : "If earliest rDzogs chen sources tend to emphasize the underlying unity of the 'minds' of buddhas and sentient beings, classical sNying thig exegetes underscored the need to establish clear priority relations between them. Their aim in doing so was to provide a framework for investigating consciousness that would allow practitioners to directly recognize (*ngo shes*) and familiarize themselves with primordial knowing (*ye shes*), the abiding condition of Mind, without confusing it with any of its derivative and distortive by-products. [...] In short, by clarifying the mind/primordial knowing distinction, rDzogs chen sNying thig scholars were in effect articulating the preconditions for the kind of knowing said to be constitutive of being a buddha (*buddhajñāna*). At the same time they were delimiting the entire range of factors that are considered obscurations and even obstacles to illumination. These so-called factors to be abandoned (*spang bya*), culled largely from Abhidharma and Yogācāra psychologies, were collectively termed 'mind' (*sems*). They are specified as what must be stopped (*'gags bya*), removed (*bral bya*) or cleared away (*sbyangs bya*) in the process known as spiritual awakening. The practical value of drawing such a distinction, then, was to illuminate how mind's self-reifying activities lead us to overlook the simple taking place of presence - open awareness or primordial knowing - in favour of the myriad perceptual and epistemic objects that claim our attention". Higgins 2012, p.64.

472 Let's note that the understanding of what needs to be purified in the approach through the fruit can also be applied to the Mahāmudrā of the *mantras* as shown by stanza 51 of the *Treatise on Pointing Out Buddha Nature* (Schaeffer 1995, note 76 p.109).

473 NT, Stanza 40.

Emptiness and Buddha Nature

At first sight, it can seem strange to claim at the same time the negation of a self and all views, and the affirmation of a Self that is rich of countless qualities. Yet, this difficulty is only apparent because this negated self is not identical to the affirmed self. Indeed, emptiness and Buddha Nature are not on the same level[474]. Emptiness negates the ordinary self, and Buddha Nature affirms the awakened self, which reveals itself after the negation of self-grasping. We are therefore in the presence of a dialectic movement, there is no contradiction between the two, but a complementarity. Buddha Nature includes and qualifies emptiness, it emphasizes the description of the absolute whereas emptiness insists more on the negation of an ordinary self. There is no difference when the mode of being of phenomena is realized. When these two aspects are taken into account, emptiness is more related to a "fundamental opening," a "native opening," freeing multiple qualities, than to a simple negation of a self. It is a fertile presence. This is then about the "Great Madhyamaka" or "supreme emptiness"[475], about the "emptiness-luminosity[476]. Emptiness is not only empty of a self[477], it is also non-empty

474 Even if the terms employed about the absolute – such as permanent or self – seem contrary to emptiness, we have already mentioned during the part on the cognitive limits of the *arhat* that they are beyond the extremes of dualistic thought (RGV I. 35-38). Additionally, we have seen that the manifestation of the absolute is necessarily a consequence of emptiness and therefore integrates it. It is also possible to find this conclusion by consulting diverse commentaries from the kagyupas masters explaining that the 3rd Karmapa was not defending a truly established permanence (see Brunnhölzl 2009, p.95-96). About this topic in other works: Ruegg 2000, p.80-81; Wangchuk 2005, p.191-194; Brunnhölzl 2009, p.67 and following. Louis de la Vallée Poussin seems to be the first one having shown these two aspects. Later, D.S. Ruegg will offer the terms "apophatic and negation" and "cataphatic et positive," in order to describe the theories *rang stong* and *gzhan stong* respectively (Wangchuk 2005, p.191). Also see Schaeffer 1995, *Chapter 5 – Apophatic and Kataphatic Tensions in the Snying bstan*, p.72-92. Besides, according to Zhönu Pal, the two last Turnings of the Wheel do not contradict each other, the only difference is that the second one does not clearly formulate the absolute (DRSM, 447.14-7, cited in Mathes 2008, p.358-359).

475 Tib. *dbu ma chen po*. On the Great Madhyamaka, see Dudjom 1991, vol. 1, pp. 178-186; Kapstein, 2000 p.106 and following.

476 We find a similar citation from Longchenpa: "Yet in contemplating that empty sky in Great Perfection meditation, the "expanse" itself lights-up in luminous vivid patterns of light unfolding from its blue essence (TDD 274.4), which indicates in a very direct way that "emptiness" is not a sterile nothingness, but rather is itself inherently overflowing with luminous light energy (such that "expanse" is more in the sense of a "dynamic filed" or "source potential" of light)". Germano 1992, p.111.

477 Tib. *rang stong* – "rangtong."

of its qualities[478]. In other words, it is only empty of otherness[479].

The manifestation of a Self is therefore not anti-Buddhist, but the natural consequence of the realization of emptiness. It is the affirmation of the inverse thesis which would be a heresy. Indeed, awakening is not an annihilation of the Self but only the negation of a certain relationship to the self and the world, thus releasing another mode of being. Recognizing the Self comes down to becoming conscious of who we truly are.

Conclusion

The teaching on Buddha Nature first of all fulfills the function of encouragement, it points to another mode of consciousness that is possible for all. Buddha Nature can inspire us, because it sparks in us a sense of trust, there is a resonance. This trust is like a propulsor, it is a positive mental event fostering awakening[480].

This teaching also allows us to complete the concept of emptiness. Indeed, Buddha Nature gives indications on what consciousness realizes once it sees emptiness. Thus, Buddha Nature is a foundation for practice in the sense that it can be compared to a traveling map where different possible states of consciousness are indicated. This prevents an interpretation that is too personal on the nature of consciousness, or a stagnation at a certain level of consciousness thinking that it is the highest one. With these indications, the practitioner discovers what is possible to realize, which prevents them from being discouraged or held back by a less rich experience. If it is correct to envision the link between Buddha Nature and meditative practice in this way, then we understand better why the qualities of consciousness are mentioned so extensively. A

478 In the *Supreme Continuum,* it is indicated that the third Turning of the Wheel has been taught to avoid the five errors. By understanding that emptiness is not empty but rich with countless qualities, the practitioner avoids the third and fourth errors, which are the "grasping of the non-real" and the "depreciation of true qualities" (RGV I. 157/136; RGV 161-165/140).

479 Tib. *gzhan stong* – "shentong." Let's note that shentong is used here in its literal sense and not with the characteristics attributed to a particular shentong like for example in the one of Dolpopa.

480 In the *Gateway to Knowledge,* trust is defined as a beneficial movement of consciousness that supports determination (*Gateway to Knowledge,* vol.1, 1.47 : *dad pa ni yang dag pa'i gnas la dang 'dod yid ches pas te 'dun pa'i rten byed pa'o*).

consciousness is perfectly awakened to the only condition that all of these qualities are present[481].

This treatise on the 3rd Karmapa also shows us that Buddha Nature is not something that is abstract or unattainable. It must be understood from the process of perception, in each moment. Each of our experiences are based on the continuum of pure consciousness, unsurpassable, which is quickly covered at the ordinary level by different mental elements, thus hiding their source. Consequently, Buddha Nature indicates that grasping is not the only way. Either our perception stays at the surface and trusts its mental formations; either it turns inwards to ascend towards the origin of its perception and develop a penetrating vision. This "ascension" is possible for all in the sense that the veils are adventitious. In contrary to Buddha Nature which is a continuum of awakened consciousness without beginning nor end, ordinary consciousness is a continuum of consciousness that is based on ignorance and can have an end[482]. On one hand, our potential is stimulated, developed, and in this case, we access profound human experiences that can take multiple shapes. On the other hand, we continue to live in a world of images, devoting ourselves to living inauthentically, which is to say in a world that does not really have true meaning.

Illusions marks a rupture with the absolute. Experience is far more profound, but ordinary consciousness tends to consider true what appears at the surface, it relies only on what is at the end of the chain. And at the end of the chain are the grossest elements, such as thoughts, emotions, "objective" knowledge... it is these different elements that rule the experience of ordinary consciousness. Being a *Buddha* in nature implies that the consciousness is richer and simpler than what it identifies with most of the time. Consciousness is not only thoughts and emotions, consciousness' nature is much vaster, it is emptiness and luminosity.

The way that we understand or consider the human being determines our way of life. Buddha Nature is therefore an essential teaching, because it shows the possibility of an existence different

481 Another possible hypothesis consists in thinking that the qualities are described by thousands so that consciousness does not lock itself onto a point of reference which shoud be reached.

482 The inseparability of knowledge and emptiness is permanent, however, the activity of the eight consciousnesses is impermanent (NT, Stanza 37-38).

from the *saṃsāra,* it offers us a refuge, from which a non-conditioned, authentic existence can bloom - one that fits us and is beneficial to all.

> Resolving doubts about the ground brings conviction in the view.
>
> Then keeping one's awareness unwavering, in accordance with the view, is the subtle pith of meditation.
>
> Putting all aspects of meditation into practice is the supreme action.
>
> The view, the meditation, the action — may there be confidence in these. *Aspiration Prayer of Mahāmudrā of Definitive Meaning,* Stanza 8.

Translation of titles in sanscrit and abbreviations

Mūlamadhyamakakārikā : *The Fundamental Wisdom of the Middle Way* (MMK)
Ratnagotravibhāga[483]: *Supreme Continuum* (RGV)
Ratnagotravibhāga-vyākhyā : *Supreme Continuum Commentary* (RGVV)

DRSM : *Theg chen po rgyud bla ma'i bstan bcos kyi 'grel bshad de kho na nyid rab tu gsal ba'i me long, Commentaire du Continuum insurpassable par Zhönu Pal (Gos lo tsā ba gzhon nu dpal)*

JOB: *The Joy of Being*

NT : *de bzhin gshegs pa'i snying po bstan pa zhes bya ba'i bstan bcos, Treatise on Pointing Out Buddha Nature*

NTC : *de bzhin gshegs pa'i snying po bstan pa'i bstan bcos kyi rnam 'grel rang byung dgongs gsal, Commentairy on the Treatise on Pointing Out Buddha Nature*

NY : *rnam shes ye shes 'byed pa'i bstan bcos, Treatise on the Distinction between Consciousness and Wisdom*

483 Tib. *rgyud bla ma*.

NYC : *rnam par shes pa dang ye shes 'byed pa'i bstan bcos kyi tshig don go gsal du 'grel pa rang byung dgongs pa'i rgyan, Commentairy on the Treatise on the Distinction between Consciousness and Wisdom*

Bibliography

Tibetan texts

Texts from the 3e Karmapa Rangjung Dorje (Rang byung rdo rje)

chos dang chos nyid rnam par 'byed pa'i bstan bcos kyi rnam par bshad pa'i rgyan, [Commentary on the Dharmadharmatāvibhāga], in *Collected Works*, vol. cha: 488–613.

dbu ma chos dbyings bstod pa'i rnam par bshad pa, dans *mngon rtogs rgyan gyi sa bcad snang byed sgron me/ sher phyin skabs brgyad kyi stong thun/ dbu ma chos dbyings bstod pa'i rnam bshad, [Commentary on the Dharmadhātustava]*, p.147-312, Vajra Vidya Institute Library, 2004.

chos dang chos nyid rnam par 'byed pa'i bstan bcos rnam par bshad pa'i rgyan ces bya ba bzhugs, [Ornament That Explains the Dharmadharmatāvibhāga], Collected Works, vol. cha., p.488-613.

nges don phyag rgya chen po'i smon lam, [Aspiration Prayer of Mahāmudrā], Collected works, Volume 11 (a).

rnam shes ye shes 'byed pa'i bstan bcos, [Treatise on the Distinction between Consciousness and Wisdom], dans mdo sngags mtshams sbyor, Volume 1 Pages 349-356.

de bzhin gshegs pa'i snying po bstan pa'i sa bcad, [*Treatise on Pointing Out Buddha Nature – Summary*]*,* dans gsung 'bum/ Collected works, Volume 7 (ja) Pages 277-281.

de bzhin gshegs pa'i snying po bstan pa zhes bya ba'i bstan bcos, [Treatise on Pointing Out Buddha Nature], dans gsung 'bum/ Collected works, Volume 7 (ja) Pages 282-290.

Commentaries from Jamgön Kongtrul (Kong sprul Blo gros mtha' yas)

de bzhin gshegs pa'i snying po bstan pa'i bstan bcos kyi rnam 'grel rang byung dgongs gsal, [*Commentary on the Treatise on Pointing Out Buddha Nature*]*, dans mdo sngags mtshams sbyor,* Volume 1 Pages 420 – 470.

rnam par shes pa dang ye shes 'byed pa'i bstan bcos kyi tshig don go gsal du 'grel pa rang byung dgongs pa'i rgyan, [Commentary on the Treatise on the Distinction between Consciousness and Wisdom], dans mdo sngags mtshams sbyor, Volume 1 Pages 357 – 412.

theg pa chen po rgyud bla ma'i bstan bcos snyin po'i don mngon sum lam gyi bshad srol dang sbyar ba'i rnam par 'grel pa phyir mi ldog pa seng ge'i nga ro zhes bya ba bzhugs so, Commentary on the Supreme Continuum, 1er volume; 182 [i.e. 363] p. W21961, karma pa chos sgar, Rumtek, 1972, Block Print.

Others

Dakpo Tashi Namgyal (dwags po paṇ chen bkra shis rnam rgyal), *nges don phyag rgya chen po'i sgom rim gsal bar bye dpa legs bshad zla ba'i 'od zer zhes bya ba bzhugs so, [Moonbeams],* Drikung Kagyu Publications, Delhi, 2004.

Gampopa (sgam po pa bsod nams rin chen), Dam chos yid bzhin gyi nor but har par in po che'i rgyan zhes bya ba bzhugs, [The Jewel Ornement of Liberation], Shri Gautam Buddha Vihara Dharma Publications, 2006.

Mipham ('jam mgon ,ju mi pham rgya mtsho), dbu ma rgyan gyi rnam bshad 'jam dbyangs bla ma dgyes pa'i zhal lung, [Commentary of Shantarakshita's Ornament of the Middle Way], Varanasi: Central Tibetan Institute of higher Tibetan Studies, 1999.

Translation of titles in sanscrit and Tibetan

Asaṅga, *La somme du grand véhicule [sct. mahāyānasaṁgraha]*, tr. Étienne Lamotte, Université de Louvain, 1973.

Candrakīrti, Introduction to the middle way: Candrakīrti's Madhyamakāvatāra, with commentary by Ju Mipham, Padmakara translation group, Shambala, 2005.

Dakpo Tashi Namgyal
— *Rayons de lune: les étapes de la méditation du Mahāmudrā*, [tib. *nges don phyag rgya chen po'i sgom rim gsal bar bye dpa legs bshad zla ba'i 'od zer zhes bya ba bzhugs so*], trad. Charrier Christian, Tsadra, 2010.
— *Moonbeams of Mahamudra*, transl. E. Callahan, Snowlion, 2019.

Gampopa
— *Le Précieux Ornement de la Libération*, [tib. *dam chos yid bzhin gyi nor but har par in po che'i rgyan zhes bya ba bzhugs]*, Padmakara, 1999.
— *The Jewel Ornement of Liberation : The Wish-Fulfilling Gem of the Noble Teachings*, Snowlion 1998.

Karmapa Rangjoung Dorjé (Troisième Karmapa)
— "Aspiration Prayer of Mahāmudrā of Definitive Meaning", in *Mahāmudrā Teachings of the Supreme Siddhas*, trans. By Lama Sherab Dorje, Snow Lion, 1995.
— *In praise of Dharmadhātu by Nāgārjuna*, [sct. *dharmadhātustotra*, tib. *dbu ma chos dbyings bstod pa*], *commentary by the third Karmapa*, [tib. *dbu ma chos dbyings bstod pa'i rnam par bshad pa*] Brunnhölzl Karl, Nithartha Institute Series, Snow Lion, 2007.
— *Luminous Heart: The Third Karmapa on Consciousness, Wisdom and Buddha Nature*, Brunnhölzl Karl, Nithartha Institute Series, Snow Lion, 2009.

Karmapa Wangchuk Dorje, *The Mahāmudrā: Eliminating the darkness of ignorance* [tib. *phyag chen ma rig mun sel*], Library of Tibetan Works and Archives, 2002, 5th edition.

The Laṅkāvatāra Sūtra : A Mahāyāna text, Suzuki, Teitaro Daisetz, Motilal Banarsidass, 2009.

Maitreya, *Maitreya's Distinguishing Phenomena and Pure being,* [sct. *dharmadharmatāvibhāga,* tib. *chos dang chos nyid rnam par byed pa],* with commentary by Mipham, Snow Lion Publications, 2004.

Maitreya & Asaṅga
— *Buddha Nature. The Mahāyāna Uttaratantra shastra with commentary.* Commentary by Jamgön Kongtrul Lodrö Thayé, explanations by Khenpo Tsultrim Gyamtso Rinpoche, translated by Rosemarie Fuchs, Snow Lion, 2000.
— *Le message du futur Bouddha ou la lignée spirituelle des trois joyaux* [sct. *Ratnagotravibhāga Mahāyānottaratantraśāstra,* tib. *rgyud bla ma*], Chenique F., éd. Dervy, 2001.

Mipham Rinpoche, *Gateway to Knowledge,* [tib. *mkhas 'jug*], Rangjung Yeshe Publications, vol. I, 1997; vol. III, 2002.

Nāgārjuna
— *Stances du Milieu par excellence,* [sct. *mūlamadhyamakakārikā],* Guy Bugault, Connaissances de l'Orient, Gallimard, 2002.
— *The Fundamental Wisdom of the Middle Way Nagarjuna's Malamadhyamakakarika translation and commentary* by Jay L. Garfield, Oxford University Press, 1995.

Saṃdhinirmocanasūtra
— *L'explication des mystères,* E. Lamotte, Université de Louvain, Recueil de travaux publiés par les membres des Conférences d'Histoire et de Philologie, 2e *Série, 34*e fascicule, 1935.
— *Wisdom of the Buddha: The Saṃdhinirmocanasūtra.* Translated by John Powers (Tibetan Translation Series 16). Berkeley: Dharma Publishing, 1994.

Śāntarakṣita; *The Adornment of the Middle way - Madhyamakālaṅkāra -*, with commentary by Jamgön Mipham, trans. by Padmakara translation group, Shechen publications New Delhi, 2008.

Śāntideva
— *Perles d'ambroisie, traduction du Bodhicaryāvatāra*, Commentaire par Kunzang Palden, Padmakara, 2006.
— *A Guide to the Bodhisattva's Way of Life*, translated by Stephen Batchelor, 1979. https://www.tibethouse.jp/about/buddhism/text/pdfs/Bodhisattvas_way_English.pdf

Books and Articles

Anālayo, *Satipaṭṭhāna: the direct path to realization,* Windhorse Publications, 2003 (2006, 2008, 2010).

Arguillère Stéphane,
— *Le vocabulaire du bouddhisme,* Ellipses, 2002.
— *Profusion de la vaste sphère : Klong-chen rab-'byams (Tibet, 1308-1364). Sa vie, son œuvre, sa doctrine.* Orientalia Lovaniensa Analecta 167, Peeters, 2007.
— *La distinction des vues : Rayon de lune du véhicule suprême,* Fayard, 2008.

Blumenthal James, *Śāntarakṣita's « Neither-One-nor-many » Argument from Madhyamakālaṃkāra (The Ornament of the Middle Way): A classical buddhist argument on the Ontological Status of Phenomena,* in Buddhist Philosophy Essential Readings, pp.45-60, Oxford University Press, 2009.

Bondolfi Guido, *Les approches utilisant des exercices de méditation de type «mindfulness» ont-elles un rôle à jouer ?,* Santé mentale au Québec, vol. 29, n° 1, p. 137-145, 2004.

Brunnhölzl Karl,
— *The Center of the Sunlit Sky: Madhyamaka in the Kagyu Tradition,* Nithartha Institute Series, Snow Lion, 2004.

— *Luminous Heart: The Third Karmapa on Consciousness, Wisdom and Buddha Nature,* Brunnhölzl Karl, Nithartha Institute Series, Snow Lion, 2009.
— *When the Clouds Part, The Uttaratantra and Its meditative tradition as a bridge between sūtra and tantra,* Snow Lion, 2014.

Bugault Guy,
— *L'Inde pense-t-elle ?,* PUF, 1994.
— *Nāgārjuna : Stances du milieu par excellence,* traduit de l'original sanskrit présenté et annoté, Connaissance de l'Orient, Gallimard, 2002.

Burchardi Anne, "The Role of Rang rig in the Pramāṇa-based Gzhan stong of the Seventh Karmapa", in: *Mahāmudrā and the Bka'-brgyud Tradition. Tibetan Studies: Proceedings of the Eleventh Seminar of the International Association for Tibetan Studies.* Ed. Roger R. Jackson and Matthew T. Kapstein. Königswinter. Andiast: International Institute for Tibetan and Buddhist Studies GmbH, p.317-344, 2011.

Chatterjee Ashok Kumar, *The Yogācāra Idealism,* Motilal Banarsidass, 1975 (second revised edition).

Demiéville Paul,
— *Le miroir spirituel,* p.145-146 dans *Choix d'études bouddhiques,* 1973.
— *Le concile de Lhasa,* Collège de France, Institut des hautes études chinoises, (1e éd. 1952) 1987.

Dhīravaṃsa, *The Middle Path of Life; Talks on the Practice of Insight Meditation,* California: Blue Dolphin, 1988 (1974).

Duckworth Douglas, *Mipam on Buddha Nature: The Ground of the Nyingma Tradition,* State University New York, 2009.

Dudjom Rinpoche, Jikdrel Yeshe Dorje, The Nyingma School of Tibetan Buddhism: Its Fundamentals and History. Trans. Gyurme Dorje and Matthew Kapstein. 2 vols. Boston: Wisdom Publications, 1991.

Dunne, John D., "Realizing the Unreal: Dharmakīrti's Theory of Yogic Perception." In Journal of Indian Philosophy 34, 2006; 497–519.

Eltschinger, Vincent, "On the Career and Cognition of Yogins." In Yogic Perception, Meditation and Altered States of Consciousness. Ed. Eli Franco. Vienna: Verlag der Österreichischen Akademie der Wissenschaften, 2009, 169–213.

Forman Robert K.C., *The problem of pure consciousness: mysticism and philosophy*, ed. by R. K.C. Forman, Oxford University Press, 1990.

Frauwallner Erich, *Amalavijñānam* und Ālayavijñānam". *Beiträge zur indischen Philologie und Altertumskunde, Walther Schubring zum 70. Geburtstag dargebracht* (Alt- und NeuIndische Studien 7), 148-159. Hamburg: Franz Steiner Verlag.

Germano David, *Poetic Thought, the Intelligent Universe, and the Mystery of Self: The Tantric Synthesis of rDzogs Chen in Fourteenth Century Tibet.* PhD. dissertation. Madison: University of Wisconsin, 1992.

Gomez Luis, "Purifying Gold: The Metaphor of Effort and Intuition in Buddhist Thought and Practice. In: *Sudden and Gradual,* p. 65-165, Gregory, Peter; ed. Sudden and Gradual Approaches to Enlightenment in Chinese Thought, Delhi: Motilal Banarsidas, 1987.

Goodman Charles, *Consequences of compassion: an interpretation and defense of buddhist ethics,* Oxford University Press, 2009.

Griffiths Paul J.,
— *Concentration or insight: The Problematic of Theravāda Buddhist Meditation-Theory,* The Journal of the American Academy of Religion, XLIX/4, p.614, 1981.
— *On being mindless. Buddhist meditation and the mind-body problem.* Sri Satguru Publications, 1999 (première édition en 1986 avec Open Court Publishing Company).

— *Pure consciousness and Indian Buddhism*, in *The problem of pure consciousness: mysticism and philosophy*, ed. by R. K.C. Forman, Oxford University Press, 1990.

Gyatso Janet, *In the Mirror of Memory: Reflections on Mindfulness and Remembrance in Indian and Tibetan Buddhism*, SUNY, 1992.

Guenther Herbert V., *From reductionism to creativity. rDzogs chen and the new sciences of Mind*, Shambala & Shaftesbury, 1989.

Harris Stephen, *Does Anātman Rationally Entail Altruism? On Bodhicaryāvatāra 8:101-103*, Journal of Buddhist Ethics, Volume 18, 2011.

Harvey Peter, *An Introduction to Buddhist Ethics: Foundations, Values and Issues*, Cambridge: Cambridge University Press, 2000.

Higgins David, *The Philosophical Foundations of Classical rDzogs chen in Tibet, Investigating the Distinction Between Dualistic Mind (sems) and Primordial knowing (ye shes)*, PhD. dissertation. UNIL, Université de Lausanne, 2012.

Hirota Dennis, "Karman: Buddhist concepts", in *Encyclopedia of Religion*, 2nd Edition Thomson Gale, Vol. 8, p. 5097-5100, 2005.

Hookham Susan K., *The Buddha within: Tathagatagarbha Doctrine According to the Shentong Interpretation of the Ratnagotravibhaga*, Sri Satguru Publications, 1991, First Indian Edition 1992.

Hugon Pascale, *Trésors du raisonnement, Sa skya Paṇḍita et ses prédécesseurs tibétains sur les modes de fonctionnement de la pensée et le fondement de l'inférence, Édition et traduction annotée du quatrième chapitre et d'une section du dixième chapitre du Tshad ma rigs pa'i gter*, Wien 2008.

Jackson David, *Enlightenment by a Single Means*. Vienna: Verlag der Österreichischen Akademie der Wissenschaften, 1994.

Jamgön Kongtrul (Le troisième), *La Nature de Bouddha : le Nyingpo Tenpa de Karmapa Rangdjoung Dordjé selon le commentaire de Lodreu Thayé*, Kunchab, 1993.

Kapani Lakshmi, La notion de saṃskāra dans l'Inde brahmanique et bouddhique, Collège de France, 1992.

Kapstein Matthew,
— "Mi-pham's Theory of Interpretation". In *Buddhist Hermeneutics*, ed. Donald Lopez. Honolulu: University of Hawai'i Press, p. 149-174, 1988.
— "We Are All Gzhan stong pas. Reflections on The Reflexive Nature of Awareness: A Tibetan Madhyamaka Defence". In *Journal of Buddhist Ethics*, vol. 7, pp. 105-125, 2000.
— *The Tibetan Assimilation of Buddhism. Conversion, Contestation, and Memory*, Oxford University Press, 2000.
— *Reason's Traces: Identity and Interpretation in Indian and Tibetan Buddhist Thought.* Boston: Wisdom Publications, 2001.
— *The Presence of Light: Divine Radiance and Religious Experience.* University of Chicago Press, 2004.
—"The Experience of Light and the Construction of Religious Experience". In *The Presence of Light*, ed. Matthew T. Kapstein, 2004.
— "Rethinking Religious Experience: Seeing the Light in the History of Religions, In *The Presence of Light*, ed. Matthew T. Kapstein, 2004.
— *The Tibetans*, Wiley-Blackwell, 2006.

Kasulis Thomas, "Nirvāṇa" dans *Encyclopedia of religion*, 2nd Edition Thomson Gale, vol.10, p.6628-6635, 1987.

Katz Steven T, *Mysticism and religious traditions*, Oxford University Press, 1978.

Kellner & Taber, *Studies in Yogācāra-Vijñānavāda idealism I: The interpretation of Vasubandhu's Viṃśikā*, ASIA 2014, 68 (3), 709-756.

Keown Damien,
— *The Nature of Buddhist Ethics*, Macmillan/Palgrave, 1992/2001.
— *Buddhist Ethics: A Very Short Introduction*, Oxford University Press, 2005.

Khenchen Thrangu, *On Buddha essence, a commentary on Rangjung Dorje's Treatise,* Shambala, 2006.

Lopez Donald S., *Interpretation of the Mahāyāna Sūtras,* In *Buddhist Hermeneutics,* ed. Donald Lopez. Honolulu: University of Hawai'i Press, 1988 pp. 47-70.

Mala Guilaine, *Empreinte du Tch'an chez les mystiques tibétains, in Tch'an, racines et floraisons,* Les Deux Océans, Paris, 1985.

Mathes Klaus-Dieter,
— "Tāranātha´s Presentation of *trisvabhāva* in the *gŹan stoṅ sñiṅ po*". In: *Journal of the International Association of Buddhist Studies,* vol. 23, no. 2, 195-223, 2000.
—"Blending the Sūtras with the Tantras: The Influence of Maitrīpa and his Circle on the Formation of *Sūtra Mahāmudrā* in the Kagyu Schools", in: *Tibetan Buddhist Literature and Praxis: Studies in its Formative Period 900-1400,* ed. by Ronald M. Davidson and Christian K. Wedemeyer (Proceedings of the Tenth Seminar of the IATS, Oxford 2003, vol. 10/4). Leiden: Brill, 201-227, 2006.
—"Can *Sūtra Mahāmudrā* be Justified on the Basis of Maitrīpa´s Apratiṣṭhānavāda?" In: *Pramāṇakīrtiḥ. Papers dedicated to Ernst Steinkellner on the occasion of his 70th birthday*. Ed. by B. Kellner, H. Krasser, H. Lasic, M.T. Much, H. Tauscher. (Wiener Studien zur Tibetologie und Buddhismuskunde, vol. 70, no. 2). Vienna: Arbeitskreis für tibetische und buddhistische Studien, 545-566, 2007b.
— *A Direct Path to the Buddha Within: Gö Lotsawa´s Mahāmudrā Interpretation of the Ratnagotravibhāga,* Boston: Wisdom Publications, 2008.
— *The Gzhan stong Model of Reality. Some More Material on its Origin, Transmission, and Interpretation,* in: Journal of the International Association of Buddhist Studies 34.1–2, 187–223, 2012.
— *A fine blend of Mahāmudrā and Madhyamaka : Maitrīpa's collection of texts on non-conceptual realization (Amanasikāra),* Wien : Verlag der Österreichischen Akademie der Wissenschaften, 2015.

Matilal Bimal Krishna, *Perception: An essay on classical Indian theories of knowledge,* Oxford: Clarendon Press, 1986.

Matsumoto Shirō, *The tathāgatagarbha theory is not Buddhist,* dans *Pruning the Bodhi tree, The storm above critical buddhism,* édité par Jamie Hubbard et Paul L. Swanson, University of Hawaï press, 1997.

O'Leary Joseph S., *Philosophie occidentale et concepts bouddhistes,* PUF, 2011.

Pettit John W., *Mipham's Beacon of Certainty Illuminating the View of Dzogchen* (Studies in Indian and Tibetan Buddhism), Somerville, Mass: Wisdom Publications, 1999.

Pol Droit R. (ouvrage collectif), *Philosophies d'ailleurs : Tome 1, Les pensées indiennes, chinoises et tibétaines,* Editions Hermann, 2009.

Powers John, *Hermeneutics and Tradition in the Saṃdhinirmocanasūtra,* Motilal Banarsidass Publishers, Delhi, 2004 (Première édition en 1993 chez Brill, Leiden).

Ratié Isabelle, *Le Soi et l'Autre: Identité, différence et altérité dans la philosophie de la Pratyabhijñā,* Brill, 2011.

Schaeffer Kurtis, *As it was Before, So is it After: A Study of the Third Karma pa Rang byung rdo rje's Treatise on Buddha Nature.* Master's thesis, University of Washington, 1995.

Scherrer Schaub, *Yuktiṣaṣṭikāvṛtti. Commentaire à la soixantaine sur le raisonnement ou Du vrai enseignement de la causalité par le maître indien Candrakīrti,* note 39, Bruxelles, Institut belge des hautes études chinoises (« Mélanges chinois et bouddhiques » 25), 1991.

Schmithausen Lambert, *Ālaya-vijñāna: On the Origin and the Early Development of a Central Concept of Yogācāra* , Philosophy East and West 43, 1993.

Seyfort Ruegg David,
— *La Théorie du tathāgatagarbha et du Gotra : Études sur la Sotériologie et la Gnoséologie du Bouddhisme* (Publications de l'École française d'Extrême-Orient 70), Paris: École française d'Extrême-Orient, 1969.
— *Le Traité du Tathāgatagarbha de Bu ston rin chen grub* (Publications de l'École française d'Extrême-Orient 88), Paris : École française d'Extrême-Orient, 1973.
— *The Meanings of the Term "Gotra" and the Textual History of the "Ratnagotravibhāga"*, Bulletin of the School of Oriental and African Studies, University of London, Vol. 39, No. 2 (1976), pp. 341-363.
— *Buddha-nature, Mind and the Problem of Gradualism in a Comparative Perspective: On the Transmission and Reception of Buddhism in India and Tibet* (Jordan Lectures in Comparative Religion 13), London: School of Oriental and African Studies, 1989.
— *Three Studies in the History of Indian and Tibetan Madhyamaka Philosophy*, Vienna, 2000.

Stearns Cyrus, *The Buddha from Dolpo: A Study of the Life and Thought of the Tibetan Master Dolpopa Sherab Gyaltsen* (SUNY series in Buddhist Studies), Albany, N.Y.: SUNY, 1999.

Swearer Donald K., "Arhat", in *Encyclopedia of Religion,* 2nd Edition Thomson Gale, p. 476-478, 1987.

Takasaki Jikido, *A Study on the Ratnagotravibhāga (Uttaratantra) Being a Treatise on the Tathāgatagarbha Theory of Mahāyāna Buddhism* (Rome Oriental Series 33), Rome: Instituto Italiano per il Medio ed Estremo Oriente, 1966.

Tarthang Tulku,
— *Time, Space and Knowledge: A new vision of reality,* Dharma Publishing, 1977.
— *The Joy of Being: Advanced Kum Nye Practices for Relaxation, Integration & Concentration,* Dharma Publishing, 2014 (1st ed. 2006); *La joie d'être,* trad. Sandy Hinzelin, Trédaniel, 2018.

Tillemans Tom J.F.
— The "neither one nor many" argument for śūnyatā and its Tibetan interpretations. In Ernst Steinkellner and Helmut Tauscher, eds., *Contributions on Tibetan and Buddhist Religion and Philosophy*, pp. 305–320. Arbeitskreis für Tibetische und Buddhistische Studien, Universität Wien, Vienna, 1983.
— Two Tibetan texts on the "neither one nor many" argument for śūnyatā. *Journal of Indian Philosophy* 12:357–388, 1984.
— Yogic Perception, Meditation, and Enlightenment. The Epistemological Issues in a Key Debate between Mādyamaka and Chan // A Companion to Buddhist Philosophy. Oxford: John Wiley & Sons, 2013. P. 290–306.

Viévard L., *Vacuité (sunyata) et compassion (karuna) dans le bouddhisme Madhyamaka*, De Boccard, 2002.

Waldron William S., *The Buddhist unconscious,* New York : Routledge Curzon, 2003.

Walpola Rahula, *L'enseignement du Bouddha. D'après les textes les plus anciens*, Points sagesses, 1961 (« What Buddha taught » : http://ftp.budaedu.org/ebooks/pdf/EN132.pdf)

Wangchuk Dorji, *The rÑiṅ-ma Interpretations of the Tathāgatagarbha Theory*, Vienna Journal of South Asian Studies 48, 171–213, 2005.

Wedemeyer Christian K. *Making sense of Tantric Buddhism: History, Semiology and Transgression in the Indian traditions,* Columbia University Press, 2013.

Westerhoff Jan, *Nagarjuna's Madhayamaka: A philosophical introduction*, Oxford University Press, 2009.

Williams Paul, *Studies in the Philosophy of the Bodhicaryāvatāra: Altruism and Reality*, Delhi, India: Motilal Banarsidass, 1998.

Zimmermann Michael, *A Buddha Within: The Tathāgatagarbhasūtra. The Earliest Exposition of the Buddha Nature Teaching in India* (Bibliotheca Philologica et Philosophica Buddhica), Tokyo: The International Institute for Advanced Buddhology, 2002.

Publishing finished
in march 2023 by Pulsio
Publisher Number: 4020
Legal Deposit: march 2023
Printed in Bulgaria